THE NEW TALIBAN: EMERGENCE AND IDEOLOGICAL SANCTIONS

THE NEW TALIBAN: EMERGENCE AND IDEOLOGICAL SANCTIONS

SYED MANZAR ABBAS ZAIDI

Nova Science Publishers, Inc.
New York

Copyright © 2009 by Nova Science Publishers, Inc.

All rights reserved. No part of this book may be reproduced, stored in a retrieval system or transmitted in any form or by any means: electronic, electrostatic, magnetic, tape, mechanical photocopying, recording or otherwise without the written permission of the Publisher.

For permission to use material from this book please contact us:
Telephone 631-231-7269; Fax 631-231-8175
Web Site: http://www.novapublishers.com

NOTICE TO THE READER

The Publisher has taken reasonable care in the preparation of this book, but makes no expressed or implied warranty of any kind and assumes no responsibility for any errors or omissions. No liability is assumed for incidental or consequential damages in connection with or arising out of information contained in this book. The Publisher shall not be liable for any special, consequential, or exemplary damages resulting, in whole or in part, from the readers' use of, or reliance upon, this material.

Independent verification should be sought for any data, advice or recommendations contained in this book. In addition, no responsibility is assumed by the publisher for any injury and/or damage to persons or property arising from any methods, products, instructions, ideas or otherwise contained in this publication.

This publication is designed to provide accurate and authoritative information with regard to the subject matter covered herein. It is sold with the clear understanding that the Publisher is not engaged in rendering legal or any other professional services. If legal or any other expert assistance is required, the services of a competent person should be sought. FROM A DECLARATION OF PARTICIPANTS JOINTLY ADOPTED BY A COMMITTEE OF THE AMERICAN BAR ASSOCIATION AND A COMMITTEE OF PUBLISHERS.

LIBRARY OF CONGRESS CATALOGING-IN-PUBLICATION DATA

Zaidi, Syed Manzar. The new Taliban : emergence and ideological sanctions / Syed Manzar Zaidi.
   p. cm.
Includes index.
ISBN 978-1-60692-882-0 (softcover)
1. Taliban. 2. Pakistan--Politics and government--1988- 3. Terrorism--Pakistan. I. Title. DS389.Z35 2009 363.325095491--dc22
                                                                                                                  2008052984

Published by Nova Science Publishers, Inc. ✦ New York

Contents

Preface	vii
Emergence	1
Ideological Sanction	29
Conclusion	55
Index	57

PREFACE

This book traces the resurgence and reorganization of the Taliban into a new organizational entity, the Taliban in Pakistan. The Taliban, forced to flee Afghanistan, have found a haven in Pakistan's tribal areas, re-organizing and recruiting anew in the process. Pakistani Taliban are ideologically similar to the Taliban in Afghanistan, but are organized in distinct organizational entities. They are, in effect, the new face of Taliban. A comprehension of the evolution of this phenomenon is a vital aid to any research into the gravity of the geopolitical situation. This study traces their evolution and ideology employed by them.

EMERGENCE

The terrorism scenario in Pakistan being constantly in a state of flux, is posing a dire threat with the gravest possible consequences to the regional socio-political stability with impending implications on the GWOT. The situation has further been aggravated by a fast developing tempo of Talibanisation, which is permeating from the tribal to the urban set-up at an alarming pace. This complexity of the situation is manifesting itself not only in socio-political and geo-strategic terms ,but is also encouraging religious extremism at the roots of tribal and urban set-up; which is unraveling immense fissiparous tendencies hostile to social fabric necessary for ensuring tolerance and spirit of peaceful co-existence in a well-organized society. This spill-over from the feudal to the mainstream of urban is changing the complexion of the latter, in so far as it is encouraging the emergence of Salafi religious ideology, which is the main driving force for the militant-Jihadi groups engaged in an endless struggle for the merger of spiritual with the temporal.

Pakistani urban society has covered a long distance over the decades, and the social change brought about is fairly well-entrenched to revert to an anti-historical past. Besides, Science and Technology have also made a lot of difference, making it well-neigh impossible to counteract the influence of Western socio-political ideology which has generally permeated the urban society. This reveals a clear paradigmatic divide between the urban educated mainstream society and a marginalized tribal one, where modern ideals are still alien to the behavioral configurations of tribalism, where this Salafi ideology is not only holding out, but gaining popularity as well. These Jihadi militant groups are staring into the eyes of socio-economic development in this region, because they have been nurtured in traditions of fundamentalism coupled with authoritarianism remaining well-protected in FATA[1] (Federally administered Tribal Areas) over ages. Waziristan (a FATA area) has been considered one of the most dangerous areas in the World by CIA, and an Al-Qaeda haven in the post 9/11 scenario, which can be a generalized statement for many of the FATA areas.[2] These areas are the birthplace of the 'New' Taliban; this is indeed resurgence, at the same time being a revival of the Talibanised form of fundamentalism which has resurfaced in Pakistan from the adjacent areas of Afghanistan. The Taliban have a new face in the form of new warlords like Baitullah Mehsud who outrivals mullah Omar in charisma. They have new sanctuaries in the form of the rugged terrain of FATA, but this is adjacent to settled cities of Pakistan which have been on the way of progressiveness. These new Taliban have found new battlegrounds in the cities and tribal areas of Pakistan, where they have started wreaking havoc with their suicide bombers. The scary aspect of this resurgence is the fact this is happening in a nuclear Islamic state which has a considerably stronger infrastructure than Afghanistan has had for decades, and the fact that these Taliban have started destabilizing a country with one of the stronger armies in the region. This is then the pinnacle of Talibanisation; it started with them entering a war ravaged country as a militia, then nearly taking over war ravaged Afghanistan, culminating in their attempt to make Pakistan a primary base for exporting their variant of extremism across the globe.

In this discourse, I have attempted to pin down the emergence of this phenomenon as a forewarning; the Taliban are far from dead. Those who insist upon this utopian thought would do well to reconsider the jubilation expressed by many scholars toward the end of the twentieth century about

---

[1] For a more detailed review of FATA, access the Government website at http://eyconsol.com/dmo/fata/index.php

[2] Anwar Iqbal "Taliban command structure in Fata alarms US", The Dawn, Dec 28,2006,access at http://www.dawn.com/2006/12/28/top1.htm

fundamentalism having spent all its steam, such as "le declin de l'Islamisme," i.e. decline of fundamentalism by the French scholar Gilles Kepel .Then 9/11 just happened to come along, reorienting, and sometimes polarizing our thought processes about what terrorism actually means to us. For the very first time, it touched the life of each and every citizen of this planet, re-shaping or concretizing our perceptions about the phenomenon. Similar sentiments to those expressed above have been expressed by observers ostensibly relieved by the defeat of Taliban in Afghanistan. "The columnist William Pfaff writes about the defeating of the Taliban in Afghanistan and argues:

> [T]he victory ... made wonderfully evident that the Islamic fundamentalism ... is a phantom. It was blown away by the first serious attack made upon it. ... This lesson inevitably will cool the attractions of fundamentalism else-where in the Muslim world."[3]

I hate to break the bad news, but it is time to wake up to the reality of Geopolitical truth of the re-organisation of Taliban. I trace the emergence of just such a phenomenon; the retreat from Afghanistan and regrouping of the fundamentalist forces in Pakistan. This is the irony of the prodigal son coming home to roost; Taliban were created by Pakistan at the behest of American CIA, and Taliban have resurfaced as the biggest danger to security of the nations of the same two nations .The name may have changed; 'Tehreek-e-Taliban-Pakistan', but the organization is undoubtedly the Pakistani home crafted version of Taliban. The jihad is now not against the Soviet Russia, but against USA and the whole of world which opposes the Talabanised version of Sharia, including Pakistani government and any other Muslim who cares to oppose them. This, then, is a clarion call to jihad; not the pedagogical sermonizing of Bin laden, but the rallying to arms of hordes of the same type of young men who brought Russia to its knees.

I have organized my discussion into sections for clarity of comprehension. The first part of the paper examines the tribalism of FATA, briefly tracing its historical evolution to its cotemporary state. An understanding of the historical

---

[3] Bassam Tibi, The Challenge of Fundamentalism: Political Islam and the New World Disorder (Berkeley and Los Angeles: University of California Press, 2002), xxiii.

dynamics of this area is vital to gain some measure of understanding of the context in which this movement has arisen. In turn, a comprehension of the civil society structure in some selected cities in Pakistan is crucial to comprehending how the spread of his movement is insidiously permeating the urban society from the predominantly rural one of FATA.I then try to shed some light on the religious convictions of the Taliban by tracing the religious indoctrination processes, languishing at some length at the Deobandi school of Islamic thought in Pakistan, and its influence on the Taliban movement. I then try to give profiles of the prominent warlords of the new Taliban. These are new faces; relative unknowns in the afghan jihad scenario but having emerged as most potent leaders in the Pakistan variation. I try to shed some light on their organizations and their terror tactics. A consistent theme throughout the whole discourse are the analogies with the afghan variant ,which I use as a benchmark for gauging the 'Taliban-ness' of the new kids on the block.

FATA AND TRIBALISM

Islamic fundamentalism should not be equated with Islam, but equally, it is a blatant lie to deny that political Islam is a major stream within contemporary Islamic civilization. The Afghan Islamists' political failure to produce realistic agendas for change[4] is a widespread phenomenon in the Muslim world. It has been called many names, some unflattering; Olivier Roy for instance calling it `the failure of political Islam'. Muslim societies seem to have been characterized in the twentieth century by two contradictory structures. The clan, tribe and ethnic group on one hand does not seem to exist in a peaceful equilibrium with the state and religion[5] on the other. Thus it is usually the small group versus the larger faith or the tribe versus the Ummah, or the religious clique against the state *which* has been the main focus of commitment, as opposed to tension against the state. This 'dualism', if you will, also manifests itself in the paradigms of Islam as opposed to Islamism or

---

[4] Ibid., ix-xxiii.
[5] Ibid.,ix.

fundamentalism. It is important to differentiate between the two; either all connections between them are cleanly severed, or they remain connected in which case Islam gets paradigmatically linked to the latter. Of course, identifying Islam with fundamentalism only adds to the intensity of the furor of Islamophobia.[6] It is this duality that I wish to sever for the purpose of this paper; Islam as a religion of peace is being overshadowed by the Islam of politics which vies against the state for expression of its grievances. This politicized religion is the religion of the old and the new Taliban. It is certainly not the idea of religion of the overwhelming majority of the citizens in the country they wish to bring under their version of Islam. This political variant is the struggle of the small tribal clique of the FATA tribals against the state which (they feel) has marginalized them. It is then a conjunction of traditional grievances, which have joined hands with the rebound phenomenon of radicalism 'coming home to roost' as it were, from neighboring Afghanistan. Thus, an insight into the tribal mindset is just as important as understanding the religious indoctrination, which has prompted the tribal lashkars (raiding parties) to take on the form of a formidable army. Let us first take a look at the evolution of FATA to its development into the 'most dangerous area' in the world.

The people of FATA and NWFP, along with sizeable populations in Pakistan's Baluchistan province and Karachi city in Sindh, account for 38-40 million people. Geographically, FATA runs north to south, forming a 1,200-kilometer wedge between Afghanistan and the settled areas of the NWFP. According to the 1998 national census, close to 3.2 million people (the current estimate is 3.5 million) live in FATA, which covers an area of 27,220 square kilometers. The Durand Line divided Pashtun tribes between British India and Afghanistan in 1893 and since then this delineation has been viewed with great contempt and resentment by Pashtuns, the peoples of FATA and NWFP. After Pakistan's emergence in 1947, this line became a major source of a tension between Pakistan and Afghanistan.

Pashtuns have been subject to invasions through out history. These included the Aryans (before 500 BC), thereafter the Achaemenians, Graeco-

---

[6] Ibid.

Scythian invasions (324-320 BC), Mauryans (313-232 BC), Greco-Bactrians (185-90 BC), and Sakas from 97 BC. During the first millennium CE, Parthians, Yue-chi (i.e. Kushans), Sassanians, White Huns and Turks followed in succession. The invaders have left their marks on the area in the form of genealogy. Many Pathans have the admixture of blood of various warriors who passed through this area, for instance, the Afridis have "an admixture of Greek blood."[7]

Briefly, the Mongols under Genghis Khan and Timur Lane managed to subdue these areas; the region which includes "Afghanistan and the North-West Frontier of Pakistan have seen perhaps more invasions in the course of history than any other country in Asia, or indeed in the world."[8] Even in the face of great armies, the Pashtuns retained their independence and fierce tribal loyalties, a source of great pride to them. If ever there was a 'warrior race', this is it.

FATA areas were once the arena for the 'Great Game' of imperial domination in the 19th century. The British colonial administrators of India tried to control them by various methods; proxy wars, installation of 'friendly' governments and direct intervention. It was vital to check the imperial bear, the Russian expansionism in Central Asia. However, the first effort at direct intervention, the fabled First afghan War, by January 1842, resulted in only one survivor, Dr Brydon, reaching jalalalabad to narrate the tragic story of the massacre of his comrades. "A large British-led army had not been wiped out so completely in living memory."[9]

There followed the Sandeman system, whose effect was the raising of tribal levies, or Khasadars, which institution survives till today. It consisted of ruling this unruly area by building roads and infrastructure with the help of local maliks, who could control the loyalties of the tribes. In return, Maliks got large grants and subsidies. However, it was not uncommon for the British friendly maliks to be seen as traitors and have an 'accident.'

---

[7] Olaf Caroe, The Pathans (London, Macmillan and Company Limited 1965)
[8] The Pak-Afghan Detente, George L. Montagno, Asian Survey, Vol. 3, No. 12 (Dec., 1963), pp. 616-624
[9] J.A. Norris, The First Afghan War 1838-42 (Cambridge, 1967).

However, even these measures failed in large part. A 'Masterly inactivity' policy was adopted in which they British administrators basically closed their eyes to the devices of the tribals, and instead concentrated on strengthening their border defenses. The British in 1901 issued a new Frontier Crimes Regulation (FCR) replacing the older generation of laws. These were an adaptation of decision making by a Jirga, a collection of tribal leaders and notables. Judicial authority was granted to the administrative officials, which tended to be British officers and/or supporters. Thus, a typical colonial device of vesting the Judiciary with the executive was introduced, so the latter could be absolutist source of power in the area. Even that did not always produce the expected results, since the political agent, a representative of the executive, frequently bought loyalties of local maliks, rather than exercising control over them. It is worth mentioning that these laws are still the law of the Tribal Areas in the form of FCR.

The FCR is a mixture of executive powers and traditional customs and norms. It has been called as the book of 'Riwaj' or local customs. It is a set of outdated and draconian laws more in tune with medieval times than twenty first century. These laws were designed to keep in subjugation people believed to be incorrigible; human rights were largely ignored and basic liberties glossed over with mentioning of abstract notions of traditions.[10]

"The most notorious sections of the regulations are 21-24 that deal with the issue of collective territorial responsibility. These are particularly problematic clauses which have empowered the political agent to punish an entire tribe or clan for crimes committed on its territory by imposing fines, arresting individuals, seizing and even demolishing property anywhere in the country."[11]

Under the FCR, the British installed political agents enjoyed the magisterial powers as well as the executive, a practice continued by the Pakistani Government. As a placating notion, however, after independence, there was a tendency to install Pashtun speaking army officers as agents. An agent had at his disposal un-audited wealth and unchecked exercise of powers;

---

[10] News on Sunday, 13-4-08, http://jang.com.pk/thenews/apr2008-weekly/nos-13-04-2008/spr.htm
[11] Ibid.

the institution gained notoriety for carrying corruption and financial well being with the perks of the 'seat'.

In 2008, with the coming into power of the new government in Pakistan, the issue of repeal of FCR was raised. Old laws become habits in FATA, and old habits traditionally die hard in this area. Many "....tribesmen are still confused over whether the FCR should be repealed or not, as they believe this would mean the extension of the Pakistani laws into the tribal society. This is not acceptable to them. Though, one thing is clear: they want an end to the unlimited powers of the political agents and support the institution of the tribal Jirga to become all powerful. They believe that Jirga is the only institution that provides for justice to the tribesmen."[12] Another tribal point of view is that the Islamic system of sharia be introduced, phasing out the FCR. There is another point of view that the Jirga should be democratically elected.[13]

On political and social issues, it is the Jirga (assembly of tribal elders) that define laws, regulations and policies. Pakistani courts and law enforcement have almost no jurisdiction over the area. As a substitute to democracy, unelected Jirga leaders from the region were invited to become full members of successive elected National Assemblies of Pakistan until 1997 to represent FATA. In 1996 the federal government of Pakistan decided to introduce adult franchise *for the first time* in the Tribal Areas for the elections held in 1997.

The society is divided into tribes. An approximate system of enumerating the tribes puts the number at around 60, but the picture is complicated by the system of sub tribal affiliations. These tend to be family affiliations as well as sub-tribal entities; the number can roughly be put at around 400 if all sub-clans are counted. The largest tribes are also the ones consistently mentioned in history; the Afridis, Achakzais, Bangash, Durrani, Khattak, Mehsuds, Mohammadzai, Mohmand, Orakzai, Shinwari, Yusufzai and Waziri.It is noticeable that Mehsuds, the tribal affiliation of Baitullah Mehsud, were renowned fighters and marksmen. Some tribes loosely affiliated themselves with the British temporarily, while others never entered into any alliance worth calling the name.

---

[12] Ibid.
[13] Ibid.

Pashtunwali is the pre-Islamic Pashtun code of conduct which regulated the intra and inert tribal dynamics. It is more of a set of principles, rather than codified laws. Honour and chivalry occupy a central theme in this tradition, along with undying loyalty to the tribe, and fierce opposition to occupation.

This code of conduct can compel a Pashtun to place all his hospitality at the door of the guest, while, 'unwelcome guests' are treated equally with violence equally passionately. Revenge is a central theme in Pashthunwali, with honor demanding a vendetta lasting sometimes for generations due to some perceived wrongdoing, usually related to honor.

FATA is an extremely poor area by any comparison. "There are few livelihood opportunities available to the people. The local economy is chiefly pastoral, with agriculture practised in a few fertile valleys. Most households are engaged in primary-level activities such as subsistence agriculture and livestock rearing, or small-scale business conducted locally."[14] In the absence of viable options to earn a living, the lure of illicit activities such as smuggling (consumer goods, weapons) and drug trafficking is as difficult to resist as the call of extremist Islamist elements."[15] "No systematic quantitative data is available on poverty. What is known, however, is that poverty in the tribal areas is high compared to the rest of Pakistan. The results of a recent participatory assessment, meanwhile, reveal the existence of a nuanced system of determining social status, involving more than a dozen classifications for poverty including miskeen (meek), aajiz (needy), ghareeb (poor), faqeer (beggar), bechara (pitiable), spera (hungry or unfortunate), tabah-o-barbad (destroyed), khwaar (frustrated) and bebakht (unlucky)."[16] It is indeed an ironic state of affairs, since the preceding information is an official version of the socio-economic indicators, provided on the Government of Pakistan's FATA website.

The Federally Administered Tribal Areas literacy rate is 17.42%, which is below the 43.92% average in Pakistan. 29.51% of the males and only 3% of

---

[14] The Government of Pakistan's official website on FATA. http://www.fata.gov.pk/index.php.
[15] Ibid.
[16] Ibid.

females receive education.[17] Electricity is free and no taxes are collected. Only about 7 % land is cultivable.

There is one hospital bed for every 2,179 people in the FATA, and one doctor for every 7,670 people. Only 43% of FATA citizens have access to clean drinking water.[18]

Now the question arises as to how and why FATA remained under complete state of isolation from the rest of the Pakistani society to the extent that the stage has reached when it has started disturbing the settled areas of the country. The roots of this variance can easily be traced back to the period of British occupation when a tacit agreement was arrived at between the British rulers and the tribals for a power-sharing formula involving the representation of tribals through a congregation of their elders known as Jirga and representation of the British Government through their state functionaries forming a part of their well-organized and well-trained Indian Political Service. This system was evolved in consequence of a process of hit and trial when the British Government realized that it was more or less impossible to maintain law & order in the settled districts like Peshawar; which were not safe from Afghan marauders indulging in loot and plunder. Tribals were paid a fixed sum for keeping the roads open and safe for travelers, and the British seldom interfered in their local customs and traditions. These arrangements were found functionally satisfactory for the maintenance of Law & order through Frontier Constabulary and Khasadars (informal paramilitary forces) taken from the tribals and forming an integral part of the Civilian Armed Forces. Thus it was left to the Indian Political Service to administer the area and to dispense justice in accordance with the Riwaj (local customs) documented in the Book of Riwaj containing legal sanctions for the implementation of this Riwaj under the necessary provisions of the above referred book. Rebellion against the British and violation of law was further encouraged due to scarce agriculture and other resources for employment; hence the Government looked the other way to smuggling and establishment of Weapon factories rampant as cottage industry for want of an alternative.

---

[17] Ibid.
[18] Ibid.

Durand frontier line between Pakistan and Afghanistan was also a nominal demarcation as the tribes were spread over the entire region both on this side and on the other side of the border towards Afghanistan. The tribals were given a safe conduct for movement across the border, and powindahs i.e. nomadic tribals moved freely across the border on both sides for search of food and shelter against the onslaughts of weather. Kabul had all along been harboring on the tunes of Pakhtoonistan with designs on the Pushtu speaking area in Pakistan. Pashtunistan (Pashto, Persian) or Pakhtunistan (Pashto, Persian, Urdu), is the idea of an historic homeland that was divided in 1893 by the Durand Line, a border between British India and Afghanistan. The Pashtuns are the largest ethnic group in Afghanistan. Pashto is the main Language spoken by 75 to 80% of people. They are concentrated mainly in the south and east. In Pakistan the Pashtuns are found in the North-West region.

Whereas Pakistan had generally been respecting Afghan sovereignty beyond Toorkham border, Afghanistan seldom spared an opportunity to interfere in Pakistan's internal affairs on the slightest possible pretext including ethnic, linguistic, and religious. These clashes were not between two sovereign states of Afghanistan and Pakistan alone, as Kabul regime had all along been mobilizing Pakistani tribals against their own state. These areas have, therefore, remained a hotbed of insurgency and Pakistan Government perforce had to stop advances of Afghan Lashkars (raiding parties) more than once after partition with India. FATA region had all along been a source of trouble due to willful violation of law, and militancy/insurgency on the part of both Afghan and Pakistani tribals. In fact it was fairly hard to distinguish between the two, because these tribals had their families and residences both in Afghanistan and Pakistan.

Thus ,it would seem logical that with a conjunction of all these factors, FATA tribal areas would be potential hotspots for any misdirected movement to entrench itself in the semi-illiterate ,economically under deprived society, whose scarce claims to affluence could be laid at the door of Weapons and Drugs Smuggling . A geographical continuity and porous borders with Afghanistan along with shared tribal and religious affiliations make these areas more akin to Afghanistan, rather than Pakistan. The existing Pak-US joint intervention in South Waziristan and Wana in the present day situation is an extension of the past, where Terrorists have found safe havens and recruiting grounds in these geographically sequestrated areas of the country. Whereas the reasons for this new development could possibly be socio-political, ethnic and/ or linguistic, but it catches on fastest if given a religious tinge. The masses can easily be exploited for want of education, and hence the suicide bombers play into the hands of their masters for revenge or exploitation of their religious feelings. The most viable educational institutions are the madrassahs since they have religious sanction behind them. The madrassahs and seminaries prepare militants and Jihadis for providing lead against the popular feeling of unfairness in the existing socio-political scenario.

There has been a physical as well as a cognitive divide between these FATA protected areas and urban ones ever since Pakistan gained independence in 1947. The transition into a FATA area from an urban one is abrupt, but beyond a flimsy physical barrier separating an urban centre like Peshawar from a FATA area like Darra Adam Khel, the world changes almost unrecognizably. The open display of Arms and ammunition is perhaps the most striking change, accompanied by a less than subtle appearance of socio-economic deprivation. Women disappear from public view more or less completely, and the area is marked by a noticeable absence of women's educational institutions, which when present, are often not well attended to. The state's writ in the form of regular Police is represented by irregular tribal levies, and in many of these areas it was often impossible much before 9/11 to enter without the permission of the Political Agent or Military/Paramilitary escort, especially for foreigners. These areas have remained relatively isolated from the rest of the society due to a strong cultural identity. This is a classic example of what social anthropologists analyzing cultural relativism interpret as a case of a culture closing[19] ranks due to the insecurity of being wiped out, but in the process, fossilizing itself to the exclusion of enlightenment. Thus, the FATA areas would seem a most logical choice for radical movements like Militant Fundamentalism to take root.

---

[19] Henry J.Steiner and Philip Alston. (2000), International Human Rights in Context: Law, Politics, morals, New York: Oxford University Press, pp.376-8.

An average urban Pakistani is averse to violence being perpetrated in the name of religion. On the other hand, we see a noticeable rise in the spate of urban suicidal bombing, purportedly as a reprisal to the US incursion and military action in the tribal belt. This complex scenario presents a blend of modernization and radical fundamentalism; wherein a marginalized local populace is reminding the party in power of its existence and fundamental rights versus the fundamentalism preached over ages. Would it be simplistic to attribute abject poverty in the tribal society as one of the important causes for the creation of terrorism? Is it incredible to understand that the children born and bred in poverty are attracted towards the religious seminaries for the provision of a square meal coupled with a guarantee for eternal life in paradise for sacrificing their life for the attainment of the objective set by a militant/terrorist religious leader? This illiterate/half-baked/semi-educated leader has a particular misdirected appreciation of religion. He sees a liberal not conforming to Ibadaat, wearing Western dress and having Western style of living, is a heretic to him; and is, therefore, Wajib-ul-Qatl[20]. His extermination is, therefore, not a loss to Islam; and hence he could possibly be eliminated without any remorse. This ideology is, therefore, resulting in a clear cognitive divide between the urban and the tribal society.

Pakistanis tend to generalize the entire NWFP as a conservative society by their own modern standards; simply by ignoring the social change brought about due to Western education creating more or less equal opportunities for either of the genders. People in the NWFP capital city of Peshawar enjoy music like any other part of the country. They wear Western dress. Women move about in socio-economic sectors relatively easily, and women's education is a given norm even in the conservative mainstream open societies in the frontier province. This way of life is under a serious threat of fundamentalism encroaching upon their lives. Another NWFP area, Swat ,was till very recently a part of the mainstream society, but in my opinion has fallen prey to extremists in Pakistan. Though conservative, it was on the pace of progress from the viewpoint of education, health, and other facilities; but of late it has adopted a path of segregation from the rest of the country in so far

---

[20] Liable to be killed without evoking any religiously generated legal sanction; a term commonly used by extremists to justify terrorism.

as their violent demand for the implementation of fundamentalism and enforcement of Sharia Law is concerned. Similar threats are now being faced by Peshawar and Karachi. The ascendancy of fundamentalism in these cities would foresee ably not be a simple process; however Peshawar seems more prone than Karachi .These tendencies are growing at an alarming rate, and nobody could have predicted a decade ago that FATA would spill over into the urban mainstream. This article is an introduction to the insidious creeping or permeation of this radical transmigration phenomenon, but I believe it has to be studied in much greater depth to provide a strategic insight as to how geographically sequestrated radical movements like the ones in FATA are starting to permeate into the urban mainstream, which is an extremely worrying trend.

THE EMERGENCE OF THE NEW TALIBAN

It would aid in the comprehension of the process of emergence of the new Taliban, to divide their evolution into chronological phases. I have no intention of going into details of how the Taliban were initially born, and what events led to their falling from grace; these can be found in a plethora of academic research, which traces this phenomenon aptly. I am more concerned with delving into the evolution of the resurgence and re-organization of the Taliban in Pakistan. This is a grey area for many of the researchers and strategists; there were early warning signs of Talibanisation of society, which tended to be dismissed by international and even local media, think tanks, and strategists as 'local disturbances' in the name of ethnicity and/or regional separatism. Certainly, the Pakistani government was understandably not very keen to admit the presence of such potential hot-spots within the society. Then, names like Abdullah, Baitullah and Fazlullah began to crop up; these were still initially dismissed as 'local' preachers or with the retort of the ages old adage about FATA: 'there have always been some unruly elements in FATA , and there will always be.' The fact that the intelligence circles realized the importance of these 'unrests' even then, is evidenced by the fact that sporadic operations against insurgency in tribal belts started as early as 2002,but these tended to be portrayed (and debatably they were ,at that that point in time) as tribal unrests.

However, the time period between 2003 and 2007 is crucial; inasmuch as these hitherto localized unrests starting gaining force; indoctrinating thousands of young men with their notions of Jihad. The movements in Swat, Bajaur and Waziristan ,all of which initially seemed to have directions of their own, started coalescing into an extremely organized guerilla movement, strikingly comparable to the birth of Taliban. That is not surprising since this movement *is* Taliban, only the Pakistani version of it as a separate organizational entity, but having the same ideological roots and Al-Qaeda connections. The formal declaration of this movement as Taliban in December 2007 may have come as a surprise to some, but for some analysts attuned to the situation, it was only a logical culmination of the state of affairs. Let us take a look at the emergence of Pakistani Taliban, which can be traced between the time quotients of 2001 and 2003.

The Pakistani support to the Taliban between the phases of 1994-2001 can be clearly documented and is a fait accompli. Regarding assistance to the Taliban, an eminent monthly periodical reported: "...there have been frequent reports of Pakistani military units offering training to the Taliban and other Jihadi groups in more than 10 training camps across Afghanistan."[21]

"The presence of professional Pakistani fighters became most obvious during the Taliban's attack on Taloqan, the capital of northern Takhar province in September 2000. There were also reports that Pakistani aircraft were used to rotate Taliban troops on the Taloqan front line. The frequency of such reports forced the UN Secretary General to implicitly accuse Pakistan of interfering in Afghanistan. The US government was also obliged to issue a demarche to the Pakistani government asking for assurances that Pakistan had not been involved in engineering, the fall of Taloqan."[22]

The New York Times claimed that Pakistan's secret services agency, the ISI, continued supplying arms to the Taliban until 12 October 2001. Quoting Egyptian and Pakistani officials, the report said: "Pakistani border guards at a check point in the Khyber pass on 8 October and 12 allowed passage to

---

[21] *The Herald*, November 2001. This is a monthly periodical published by the Dawn group of Newspapers.
[22] Ibid.

convoys of trucks loaded with rifles, ammunition and rocket-propelled grenade launchers hidden under their tarpaulins headed into Afghanistan."[23]

"A senior Pakistani intelligence official acknowledged that the 8 October shipment did contain arms for the Taliban. But the official also said it was the last officially sanctioned delivery and that Pakistan had since been living up to its commitment to the anti-terror war."[24]

The Herald wrote further regarding the supply of arms to the Taliban by the ISI "The shipment of fresh weapons supplies to the Taliban from Pakistani territory continued through subsequent years. During 1994-96, these supplies passed through the Kurram Agency (a tribal area) and were delivered at various locations up to Khost in southern Afghanistan.

"Later, the route shifted to the main border crossing on Torkham and the deliveries were made directly to the central corps headquarters in Kabul.[25] Till 2002, there were well documented reports of Pakistani presence in Afghanistan, a fact which seemed to have been hushed up after 2002.

For example, an extract from a news report[26] about an interview with a soldier covertly infiltrating Afghanistan states "All these men (the mujahideen) had reached there with the help of the Sakhi Ehsan Mosque which is run in Karachi with assistance from the al-Rasheed Trust. In all, there were 2000 Pakistanis and 400 Arabs there."

Why did Pakistan want to keep on supplying Taliban even after they had failed in Afghanistan? It seems that the continued ability to exert influence in the region was important to the establishment. Confirming this view, Jessica Stern wrote in the American Foreign Affairs magazine' in December 2001: "Pakistan has two reasons to support the so-called mujahideen. First, the Pakistani military is determined to pay India back for allegedly fomenting separatism in what was once East Pakistan and which in 1971 became Bangladesh. Second, India dwarfs Pakistan in population, economic strength, and military might. In 1998 India spent about two per cent of its $469 billion GDP on defense, including an active armed force of more than 1.1 million

---

[23] *The New York Times,* 8 December 2001.
[24] Ibid.
[25] (Herald, Nov. 2001)
[26] The Friday Times, Lahore, 10 December 2002.

personnel. In the same year, Pakistan spent about five per cent of its $61 billion GDP on defense, yielding an active armed force only half the size of India's. The US government estimates that India has 400,000 troops in Indian-held Kashmir – a force more than two thirds as large as Pakistan's entire active army. The Pakistani government thus supports the irregulars as a relatively cheap way to keep Indian forces tied down."

Another reason postulated was that the newly installed Karzai regime was largely seen by Pakistani intelligence circles as pro-India, and was also considered by many circles to be anti-Pakistan. Pakistani strategists wanted to counter his influence in the region by keeping the Taliban primed to keep the Karzai government in check.

The Taliban, though seemingly defeated in Afghanistan, had not entirely lost their support in the region. As will be elaborated upon later, the all powerful ISI had strong ties with them, even though the president in 2002 had distanced himself from the extremists. According to Zarb-*e-Momin*[27], a Jihadi periodical, the Taliban were said to have regained control of more than forty districts of Afghanistan. It is probable that sometimes Jihadi magazines tend to propagandize more than reporting facts, but, even then, it was conjectured at that time that Pakistani forces were behind this operation. Evidence of this seems to come from the fact that groups of twenty to thirty Taliban and Al-Qaeda at a time, were infiltrating into Pakistan from the afghan side, even though seventy thousand Pakistani troops were guarding the border (The Daily Times ,Lahore, 20 July 2002). Most of this infiltration occurred in the tribal belts of FATA, where the indigenous tribes were sympathetic to the cause of the Taliban and other Jihadi groups. As mentioned above, the tribals have little love for strangers; the Pashthunwali code binds them in much stronger ties to the Taliban which had been permeating the borders at that time. These boys were heroes in the eyes of the tribals; they had brought down the Soviet bear, and had withstood the onslaught of the allied forces with hugely smaller resources. Besides, they were known compatriots, who had been coming and going as they pleased during the afghan Jihad days. Most of the infiltration occurred in North and South Waziristan, Bajaur Agency,

---

[27] Zarb-e-momin, 11 December 2003.

Bannu, and Dera Ismail Khan. It is not surprising that the current insurgency is at its worst in Waziristan and Bajaur areas. *Nidai Millat* catalogues such an event: "When the Americans bombarded Tora Bora at the very beginning of their aggression on Afghanistan, the Arab Mujahideen left the place and sought refuge with the tribals in Chinar tribal areas. They had to set out again after getting back to health but just two days later, another rival tribe came to know of their refuge there, and they informed the Americans and Pakistani forces of their presence there. According to the tribals of Para Chinar, just as they got this information, the Americans started pressurising the Pakistan government to interfere into the matter. According to sources, the Pakistani officials started holding talks with the seniors in the tribe."[28]

The Washington Post in 2003 published an interview with a Pakistani tribal, showing the extent of the tribal affiliation with the Taliban: "Abdul Zahir and 14 other Pakistanis set out by bus for Afghanistan last summer, determined to join Taliban forces waging a renewed jihad against US and Afghan Government troops. It was almost too easy. Stopped by border guards in the town of Chaman, they said they were Afghan refugees returning home on various personal or business errands. Zahir said: `I said I sold a buffalo to someone in Afghanistan and I needed to collect my money.' The guards waved them through. A few days later, he and his comrades joined a Taliban unit in the mountains of Zabol province. They were issued weapons and spent the next 40 days engaged in sporadic combat ... it's no problem to cross back and forth,' said Zahir, a 33-year-old apple grower and self-described Taliban recruiter from the remote tribal district of Qua Abdullah along the Afghan border in northern Baluchistan Province. The Americans have robbed us of the right to live, but still we have the right to die, and we are using that right."[29]

"That is more or less the picture sketched by Zahir, a father of six with a 10th grade education who makes his living off the 30-acre apple orchard he owns with relatives just a few miles from Afghanistan in Qila Abdullah. A Pushton tribesman, he said he identifies more closely with Afghans than with Pakistanis and first offered his services to the Taliban soon after the United

---

[28] Nidai Millat, Lahore, 19 September 2002.
[29] The Washington Post, 20 October 2003.

States launched its campaign against the movement in the fall of 2001. He joined a Taliban unit in the Afghan provincial capital of Kandahar, he said, and was promptly dispatched to the city of Mazar-eSharif as part of a mission to deliver money and winter clothing to Taliban forces there............After I came back I was continuously trying to go back, but the jihad had not yet resumed,' he said. In February, Zahir said, he succeeded in meeting a Taliban military commander who `realised I was a genuine person' with ties to the movement and urged him to `go back and convince other people' to join the jihad. Over the next few moths, Zahir said, he rounded up 14 other men from his village and surrounding areas while he waited for further instructions.....Once he got home, Zahir said, he resumed his recruitment drive and soon lined up six more Pakistanis - four madrasa students, one farm worker and an English-speaking computer expert - between the ages of 22 and 30. He said jihad is an easy sell where he lives. `We are basically anti-American,' he said. So what I do is I go and tell these boys, `The door for jihad is open and let us go fight Americans."[30] This report demonstrates where the sympathies of the regional population in the Frontier Province and the tribal areas lie. But it is not just in these areas that the Taliban and Jihadi groups have support. They have sympathizers all over Pakistan among the general population. The Afghan Taliban gets most of their volunteers from Afghanistan itself, but has now opened a 'chapter' so to speak, in Pakistan. The Karzai regime is purportedly controlling the country in Afghanistan, but in reality, is only in control in Kabul and the previous Northern Alliance areas of the country.[31] According to some reports, the Taliban have a continued presence in most of the country.[32] At the same time the allies in Afghanistan seem to have fallen back to a precautionary approach towards the Taliban. The American and Allied Forces seldom seem to make large incursions into the mountains, relying mainly on consolidation and caution rather than attempt making large inroads into the territory still containing small guerilla groups of Taliban. This is evident from a reading of the following report from *The Washington Times:* "US commanders have turned down as too risky plans for

---

[30] Ibid.
[31] Chris sands "Afghanistan; is it too late?" New Statesman, 31 March 2008.
[32] Ibid.

special operations missions to attack Taliban and al-Qaida fighters in Afghanistan, according to soldiers and Bush administration officials. Military sources said that on several occasions, Army Green Beret A-Teams received good intelligence on the whereabouts of former Taliban leader Mullah Mohammad Omar, one of the United States' most sought after fugitives. In each case, soldiers said, commanders turned down the missions as too dangerous or because they believed the intelligence was shaky. … `We had a good plan,' said one Special Forces soldier, who, like others interviewed for this story, asked not be identified for fear of retribution from superiors. We came in hard in November December, January, February and we won,' the soldier said. `Since then, we've been floundering.' … intelligence collected by A-Teams and US agencies, there are likely only 50 to 100 devoted Taliban leaders left in Afghanistan. Some are trying to form new guerilla groups by merging with Pakistani and Arab militants." Special Forces soldiers on the ground say that if the United States misses its chance now to kill or capture them, the hard-core Taliban leaders may be successful in reorganising their units and other militants … . "It seems that the Taliban have sound strategists; they *have* reorganized themselves, but in Pakistan.

The Taliban are primarily guerilla fighters, which invariably need a base to recuperate, train, and reorganize. The Taliban have found that base in tribal Pakistan. It would be pertinent to examine the elements of support within the Pakistani society which contributed to the rise of the 'Pakistanized' version of Taliban.

Even after Pakistan had officially withdrawn its support from Taliban after the initiation of American attacks; the situation on ground remained different. Prominent journalist and Afghan authority Ahmed Rashid, wrote in the Daily Times newspaper on 25 July 2003: "Afghanistan suspects the Pakistani leadership has resumed providing covert support to the radical Islamic movement. Some diplomats contend that President Musharraf, his army and the powerful security agency known as Inter-Services Intelligence (ISI), are directly supporting the Taliban as a matter of state policy. Musharraf's personal denials of such claims now carry little weight with Kabul's diplomatic corps. Even a boost from President Bush, who Musharraf met with in June, has been unable to dispel diplomatic scepticism. American officials are among those calling on Musharraf to step up anti-terrorist efforts. `Every effort has to be made by Pakistan not to allow its territory to be used by Taliban elements,' said Zalmay Khalilzad, the American special envoy to Afghanistan at a press conference on 15 July. `We need 100 per cent assurances on this from Pakistan, not 50 per cent assurances,' Khalilzad added, `We know the Taliban are planning and organising in Quetta."[33]

Suspicions about the Pakistani establishment harboring the Taliban have always been rampant. However, post 2002; the official stance has been to decry any involvement. That official patronage of Taliban may be a fact or fiction, but it is logical to assume that at least the ISI had not lost its previous hold over the Taliban, a fact borne out by recent reports of American pressure being exerted upon the Pakistani government to rein in the ISI. It is worth mentioning that even though Pakistan's military regime arrested some five hundred members of al-Qaida in Pakistan, not a single Taliban leader was apprehended in that period.

Many tribals on the Pak-Afghan border, undoubtedly, have been engaged in helping with the reorganization of the Taliban, and much evidence is available to substantiate this. Al-Hilal (a Jihadi periodical) of a Jihadi organization Jamiat-ul-Ansar wrote in its September 2003 issue: "It is not easy to have access within a difficult area like Waziristan. According to President Musharraf, we won this area where (previously) the army could not enter for a hundred and fifty years. But why couldn't this army stay on after crossing over Kargil? He may not like to answer this question because it was done on the orders of an `ally'. It is not easy for Pakistani officials to stand by the promises made. Posts were established to stop the Taliban but the area of operations remained rather limited. The doorway into Afghanistan cannot be stopped even by America, not to talk of Pakistan. On the one hand, the long stretch of this border is a cause for the impossibility to stop infiltration, while on the other, there are fighting tribals on both sides who also happen to be relatives of each other. They have a tradition of being warm to the guests and remain united against the aliens. The strength of the states of Khost and Paktia in

---

[33] Daily times 25, July 2003.

Afghanistan is also because of their physical proximity with Waziristan. Famous Taliban commanders, Jalaluddin Haqqani and Saifulla are popular in countless households. They are not strangers for the Taliban; in fact they happen to be their kith and kin. They have a history of their own. They did not allow the British to enter their areas by waging guerilla war. The story of Russia is too fresh in memory. An army may stand in the battleground only when they have the support of the people."

Even if some of the discourse above could be dismissed as rhetoric, there is certainly an element of support for the Jihadis from within the tribal belts. It would not have been otherwise possible for thousands of volunteers of the Sufi Mohammad movement, called Tehreek-e-Nifaz-e-Shariat-Mohammadi (TNSM), to enter Afghanistan in October 2001 to help the Taliban. (Sufi's son in law, Fazlullah is playing a tremendous part in shaping the 'New' Taliban, as I will show later) When they returned home, many members of al-Qaida and the Taliban returned with them to the tribal areas. In fact, some reports claim that Osama bin Laden, disguised in tribal garb, had also arrived with them in mid-November 2001.

Taliban have also been arriving in the province of Baluchistan in strength from neighboring Afghanistan. Quetta and the neighboring city of Chaman have become new establishments for the Taliban. Syed Salim Shahzad, a Karachi based journalist and researcher wrote in *Asia Times* after his tour of Chaman: "Immediately after entering the centre of Chaman *city,* located in Pakistan's Baluchistan province in southwest Pakistan right on the border with Afghanistan, a road curves left into the dusty distance. It leads to a chain of villages scattered along the border, some in Pakistan, some in Afghanistan, some spread across both countries, and all staunchly Pushton - and tribal - before anything else. Chaman…. is a completely mullah-dominated society." Shahzad elucidates the only means of education in the area. "Islamic seminaries (madrasas) provide an ideal way out for providing education, especially when the ideology, food, facilities and education are all free, and in some cases they even pay their students a stipend for pocket money. No wonder that they are popular." He also sheds light on how the emergence of Taliban has affected these areas. "...after the emergence of the Taliban the situation changed upside down. The Taliban heavily influenced the politics of the area and the people were influenced by their Islamic ideologies. As a result, donations were showered on the Jamiat Ulema-e-Islam (a Pakistani organization ideologically associated with the Taliban movement) which then established a network of Islamic schools and which had funds to operate them. Now, sometimes in a single village, there are two Islamic seminaries, and I think the total number in Chaman and the villages around it comes to 200, with at least 50 students in each seminary. This is the real fuel for the Taliban (resistance) movement in Afghanistan and for the fighters of the Taliban."

Journalist Ahmed Rashid also wrote in The Daily Times on 28 January

> 2004 about this Taliban resurgence in Baluchistan: "Pakistan's Jamiat Ulema-e-Islam (JUI) party now forms part of the governing coalition that rules Baluchistan. It is using its madrasas and mosques to house and mobilize thousands of a new, even younger, generation of Afghan and Pakistani Taliban to fight the Karzai government and terrorize southern Afghanistan. After prayers are over, the young Taliban - many of them in their teens - flood into the tea stalls of Pushtonabad, a Quetta suburb, in their distinctive black clothes, black turbans, long beards, and unkempt hair. They talk of the progress of the Taliban offensive in Afghanistan today. Taliban fighters, I was told, are better equipped than they were in 1994. They are buying Thuraya satellite telephones and hundreds of Honda motorbikes to carry out guerilla raids; they are also importing night-vision equipment from the Arab Gulf states."

Any account of the rise of Pakistan's Taliban will not be complete without mention of the Jihadi groups in Pakistan. Pakistani Jihadi groups and the Taliban are inextricably linked; in fact many of them have lost their separate identities and now *are* Taliban. This should be unsurprising to any analyst covering the afghan conflict, since these organizations have always played an important part in the afghan jihad. Several had safe houses in Peshawar where Mujahideen would come to take respite from the rigors of war. Similarly, many of these organizations gained their training in camps in Afghanistan such as the Sarobi and Jyora camps in Khost, the Ghazni training centre in the Shahshgoo Hills, the Mohammad training centre in Bangarbar, the Rashkor camp to the north of Kabul and the Karaga camp to the west of Kabul. At times the number of Pakistani Mujahideen at a particular front greatly outnumbered the Afghans.

Shamsheer (a Jihadi periodical published from Hyderabad in Pakistan) in its April 2002 issue, quoted one Pakistani Mujahideen activist as saying: "All of us were Pakistanis. There were two Taliban fronts nearby and close to the Amu river were the fronts of the Arab mujahideen. On the Arab fronts there were no mujahideen from any other country." It would be too much to expect that such close ties of the Jihadis with the Taliban would be severed after the fall of Kabul. In fact, it seemed obvious from doing a literature review of Jihadi publications, that these organizations were preparing for a 'new' jihad after the fall of Kabul; this would inexorably lead to the Taliban taking centre stage at the Pakistani militant scene.

Al-Irshad, a Jihadi periodical for instance, published the following message from the Emirs of Harkat-ul Jihad-ul-Islami after the fall of the Taliban: "Victory shall be with those who are in the right (God willing). The mujahideen should work in a better manner now; they should sacrifice their lives and property to be dear to God. Harkat-ulJihad-ul-Islami is devoting all its strength on this occasion and we hope that the mujahideen and the workers too will do their best."

"An activist of the Harkat-ul-Mujahideen, who has been involved in Afghanistan since 1988, concurs with the contention that, ` They maintain that there are hundreds of thousands of people, particularly from Baluchistan, the Frontier Province and the tribal belt who have committed themselves to the jihad when the call comes. In fact, in many villages in the Frontier Province and Baluchistan along the Afghan border families deem it their religious duty to send a loved one to fight in the jihad."[34]

"It is clear from these various reports that Pakistani Jihadi groups are taking part in the new jihad against America and the Northern Alliance alongside al-Qaida and the Taliban. The prominent Pakistani groups making their contributions include: Harkat-ul-Mujahideen (Jamiat-ul-Ansar), Harkat-ul Jihad-ul-Islami, Jaish-e-Mohammad, Jamiat al-Furqan, Jamiatul-Mujahideen, al-Badr Mujahideen and Lashkar-eTaiba. Reliable Jihadi sources admit that the Jihadi organizations are winding up their base camps in

---

[34] Amir Rana, The seeds of Terrorism (London: New Millennium Press, 2005), 242.

Kashmir and moving them to the Afghan border regions. These mujahideen have moved especially to assist the Taliban."[35]

I tend to subscribe to the viewpoint which is gaining currency in strategic circles; Pakistan, rather than Afghanistan, is the nucleus for indoctrination, training and radicalization of the Sunni brand of militant Islam, which envelops Taliban and other Deobandi entities in its fold. These entities had an inclination to be elitist; membership was granted on basis of a particular narrowly defined ideological mindset .However, the scenario seems to be changing, with the emergence of Taliban complicating an already explosive situation. These militants have joined hands under the banner of Taliban. Even the Afghan militant parties seem to be gravitating towards Pakistan.

A case in point would be the ultra radical ex Prime Minster of Kabul Gulbeddin Hikmetyar. According to The Daily Times (7 December 2003), Hikmetyar and his organization has been subsumed into the larger Taliban organization. The Hizb exerted tremendous influence on the Pashtuns of the tribal belts, spurred by shared ethnicity and Islamist ideals. There are unsubstantiated reports that he is in contact with the pro-Wahabi Abdul Rasul Sayyaf.[36] Hikmetyar's last public appearance in Pakistan was recorded at the annual al-Badr convention at Mansahra in February 2003; Al-Badr being a subsidiary Jihadi organization of Jamaat-e-Islami. Al-Badr had taken part in the jihad against Soviet forces along with Hizb-e-Islami.

The Daily Times article continues: "Significantly, in the early 1980s, these Afghan leaders, including Hikmetyar, belonged to the Muslim Brotherhood which emerged out of the Arab world and was the precursor to today's more extreme Islamic movements. Hikmetyar is trying to revive those connections and propagate Muslim Brotherhood ideology which is stridently anti-Western and anti-democratic. He says; `All true Muslim Afghans who want an Islamic government in their country must know it is possible only when the United States and Allied soldiers are forced out."

"Hikmetyar is also trying to whip up the sentiments of Pushton nationalism. In cassettes sent to journalists· he accuses the United States and the Kabul government of beginning `a genocide on the Pushtons' He has a

---

[35] Ibid., 243.
[36] The Daily Times,7 December 2003.

considerable network of supporters in Pakistan. After the 1979 Soviet invasion, the ISI promoted Hikmetyar ruthlessly, until he was dumped in favour of the Taliban in 1995."[37]

"Anger against the army runs high among deeply conservative tribesmen in this tribal zone that both Kabul and Pakistan suspect to be safe havens for Taliban and al-Qaida elements, but tribal chieftains avoid open criticism of the army."

"However, younger tribesmen are more vocal about their feelings. `Everyone is sad about the operation conducted against our people,' 28-year-old taxi driver Wahidullah told a newspaper (The Daily Times 16 October 2003). `Some day *our people might attack the army*[38] if such operations continue,' he warned."

Al Qaeda and Taliban have gained enormous organizational strength during the period from 2003-2007.It seems probable that they had help; the kind of military organization displayed by militants in the current insurgency in the tribal areas smacks of significant logistical and financial support. Fingers have always been pointing at the ISI, but China and Russia have been named as well; getting revenge for the soviet rout by destabilizing the Americans prompting the previous combatants to become allies (Nidai Millat, 19 September 2001). Conspiracy theories abound at this moment in time, however, and substantiation of these allegations has not been forthcoming.

This emergence of Taliban in Pakistan has unfolded a complexity to the already changing socio-political, socio-cultural, and socio-economic scenario; thus confronting Pakistan with a situation, in which their former allies were in a state of flux, and had started posing threats to regional geopolitical situation. Initially the Government of Pakistan failed to realize the gravity of this situation, but has now been jolted out of this slumber with writing on the wall 'Act immediately or you will perish by the time-lag which you failed to appreciate in time'. Hence it is time to take appropriate physical measures (such as preparedness to confront aggression), socio-cultural measures (such as ensuring that these Taliban are not accepted by Pakistani tribesmen as brothers in faith and hence providing impetus for their revolt against their own

---

[37] Ibid.
[38] Emphasis added by author.

country), socio-political measures (i.e. taking measures to step-up spirit of Pakistani nationalism which has been ignored so far) and befitting socio-economic measures to keep them away from our own soil. Unless this task is accomplished, the scenario does not present a happy picture for domestic or international stability. It is time to act - the sooner the better.

IDEOLOGICAL SANCTION

The mythos of jihad evolving into the 'neo-logos' of terrorism predates Bin Laden. Early echoes resonate in the risalat aljihad/"essay on jihad," written by Hassan al-Banna. His Muslim Brothers initiated the now characteristic patterns of slaughter, which induced chaos at a domestic level. Bin Laden it internationalized it. The Taliban in Afghanistan gave it the shape of a 'neo-Jihadi-state' out of the chaotic scenario they inherited .The new Taliban in Pakistan are in the process of destabilizing a hitherto consolidated nation state in Pakistan ,to create a state of chaos in an attempt of re-integration in the Taliban model.

Qutb and al-Banna provided the ideological substrate on which Maudoodi built up, and later 'neo-scholars' followed. This is the kind of dogma which would eventually get preached in the FATA areas in Pakistan, which would come under the ideological sway of a distilled radicalism attracted by the Afghanistan Jihad. This is the intellectual doctrine of the Taliban, who would imbibe a highly distorted version of it to get inspired in madrassahs in Pakistan to go and fight in Afghanistan. It is essential to grasp the dynamics of the three types of movements in the Islamic paradigm, which have had significant impact on shaping the ideology of the Taliban. These are the Muslim brotherhood, the jamaat-e-Islami, and the Deobandi school of thought encompassing within it the Jamiat-ul-ulema Islam, the surrogate parent of

Taliban. At the outset, however, I would like to clarify that the Taliban do not subscribe to any one of the philosophies in particular; theirs' is a hybrid all of their own. However, it is necessary to examine all three movements briefly because the Taliban ideology claims to trace its lineage and/or religious legitimacy from them, in one form or the other.

The Jamaat-e-Islami was the first organization in Pakistan to establish itself in a religio- political sense; being inspired in turn by the Ikhwan ul Muslimeen, or the Muslim Brotherhood which was set up in Egypt in 1928 with the aim of bringing about an Islamic revolution and creating an Islamic state. The founder of the Ikhwan, Hasan al-Banna (1906–1949) was a major influence on Abul-Ala Maudoodi (1903–1978), who founded the Pakistani Jamaat in 1941. It would be worthwhile briefly retracing the history of jamaat, to comprehend the thought process that would later go into molding the minds of the young Taliban.

The Jamaat-e-Islami was founded on the 25th August, 1941, in Lahore. From the very inception, the emphasis was much more on religion than politics; the independence movement for creation of the nation state of Pakistan was in full swing at the movement, but the founding constitution makes no mention of it. Maulana Maudoodi was elected as the Amir of the Jamaat. The central theme was organizational; "Although there are many individuals who have been working in the Path of Allah, they should understand that for those who have one purpose and one ideal to remain isolated is not only wrong in principle, but also is unprofitable in practical terms."[39] The jamaat has been consistent to this theme of organization; it is still one of the most organized political organizations in Pakistan, able to rally support of thousands of followers with seemingly little effort for its frequently announced rallies and 'long marches'.

Pan Islamism has also been a consistent theme behind the reason of existence of the jamaat. Maudoodi at its' inception said; "The idea on which the constitutional foundation (of the Jamaat) has been placed is that we should not only strive for the realization of one single aspect of Islam or talk of one single aspect or the religious ideals of the Muslims, but should stand for Islam

---

[39] Tarjuman-ul-Qur'an, Vol. 18. No. 2, p. 13.This is the official periodical for the organization.

as a whole, The purpose for which Prophets have come to the world should be our purpose. We should reiterate the invitation given by them, and the methods which they used to make a congregation of their followers—"[40]

The recurring theme in the founding constitution of the Jamaat-e-Islami is personal righteousness; no mention can be found of an Islamic State or the modalities of its founding. For that matter, there is little stress on politics, the discourse being more of an evangelical nature. Both these objectives would later get incorporated in the manifesto.

The constitution comprises eleven clauses which are listed under six subjects: the first subject is Aqida (Belief or faith), containing only one clause. It reads: "The basic term of faith of the Jama'at-i-Islami is that "There is no god but God, and Muhammad is His Messenger"." The constitution then discusses the full scope of the Kalima Tayyiba and explains that to consider any one but God as the object of worship places a man out of the pale of Islam. The second clause enjoins members to forget notions of nationalism, race, colour, etc., and become united in Allah's cause. The third and fourth clauses deal with the credentials of potential members. Puritanical attitudes are stressed, along with rejection of member status for persons serving under governments which recognize sovereignty other than of God. The total membership of the Jama'at-i-Islami before partition of India, however, did not rise to more than about 500, although its sympathizers may have had a higher number. There is no way to ascertain the exact number of sympathizers now, but a safe bet would be in hundreds of thousands. Membership, however, continues to be judged by the same stringent standards, using almost brutal thoroughness. A man may toil for years, to prove himself worthy of membership before he can be accepted in the ranks of the party.

The Ikhwan was established at Ismailiya by Sheikh Hasan al-Banna in 1928, but it was not until the late thirties that its programme developed. The Ikhwan Islamicists refused to compromise with the indigenous neo-colonial elite, and wanted radical political change, which rejected nationalism, ethnicity, tribal segmentation and feudal class structures in favour of a new Muslim internationalism reuniting the Muslim Ummah. Organizations

---

[40] Ibid., p. 14.

inspired by the Muslim brotherhood have thus strived to achieve this high level of organizational hierarchy demanded by the mandate, to combine military like organization along with political acumen. Pakistani Jamaat and Hikmetyar's Hizb-e-Islami ,along with setting up highly centralized modern parties ,have simultaneously worked on paramilitary lines with cells, extreme secrecy, political indoctrination and military training as part of their training programme[41]. It is pertinent that both the Jamaat and the Hizb were in intimate contact during the Afghan jihad days. The Hizb has been since subsumed within the larger Taliban umbrella body.

These are not the only parallels between the Jamaat and Ikhwan. Both parties had been engaged in translation of the literature of the other into their own respective languages, and disseminating the translated works widely.

An example is the widely disseminated translation of a lecture by Banna in 1938, quotation of excerpts from which will illustrate the similarity of thought process between them.

Shaikh Hasan al-Banna mentions in the beginning the rationale for his organization: "This was the firm ideal on which we had all agreed, that each one of us will strive towards our goal, of redirecting public opinion as a whole towards the right Islamic viewpoint." He continued, "The foundation, the thought and the goal are Islamic and they are Islamic only. The organization does not have a single iota in common with non-Islam."[42] Similar words can be attributed to Maulana Maududi at the time of the establishment of the Jamaat-e-Islami said; "We have stood for the real Islam and only for Islam, and our movement is to include the whole of Islam."[43]

As regards the universalism of Islam Maududi said, "Islam is for all humanity, and all those things which are in any way related to man are connected with Islam, so that the Islamic Movement is a movement which is all embracing...it has to change the whole pattern the world. We are following the correct religion which was established by the Prophet of Allah (peace be upon him and his followers)".[44] In the lecture mentioned above, Hasan al-

---

[41] Ahmed Rashid, Taliban: The story of the Afghan Warlords(London: Pan Macmillan Ltd, 2001), 86.
[42] Mukhtasar Tarikh-i-Ikhwan-al Muslimun (Jamaat-e-Islami, Lahore, n.d.) pp. 1-2.
[43] Tarjuman-ul-Qur'an, September 1941, p. 5.
[44] Ibid.

Banna strikes upon the same note: "Islam", he says, "is a complete religion which has in its purview the solution of all problems of man for every age...it is our belief that the tenets of Islam are related to both this world and the world hereafter...the truth is that Islam is a belief, as well as a prayer, it is nationality as well as race, it is din (religion) as well as State, it is spiritual as well as mundane."[45]

As a further similarity, both these religious parties have used similar methods on coming down to the level of mundane politics. They have both taken part in the elections of their respective countries. The jamaat did surprisingly well in the previous elections in Pakistan, where they loosely shared power with other Islamist parties under the banner of Muttahida Majlis-e-Amal.(MMA)However, they did not fare well at elections in 2008, losing majority of their seats. It is worthwhile mentioning that much of their current clout has arisen under the leadership of Qazi Hussain Ahmed, a figure nearly as revered by jamaat workers as Maudoodi.

Coming back to the Jamaat's ideology, Maudoodi, like Rashid Rida, makes frequent hostile mention to the western civilization in his writings. However, he admits the challenges faced by Islam against the modern world in the face of scientific advancements, mentioning that these can assist in the recovery of his country and hence Islam.

As regards Jihad, Maudoodi's concept of it is contained in two important works, namely Al-Jihad fil-Islam, first published in 1930, and a smaller book entitled Jihad-i-fi sabilillah. A detailed discussion would be beyond the scope of this study; suffice it to say that the most controversial of his interpretative discourses on jihad is that the Muslims should declare Jihad against only those infidels who prevent the truth of God from prevailing in the world.[46] The obvious problem is that his condition could be interpreted in a very loose sense, which it has tended to be done by fundamentalists seeking religious sanction for their militancy.

Maududi does qualify his view by a pre-condition; it can be applied only in the case of those non-Muslim states which have done wrong to the Muslim community. However, interpreted loosely, its ambiguous assertions could be

---

[45] (Mukhtasar Tarikh-i-Ikhwan-al-Muslimun, Jamaat Islami), p. 3.
[46] Maududi, Al jihad flu Islam, (Islamic Publications Ltd., Lahore, 1962), pp. 48-50.

applied to any non-Muslim state. This aspect of Jihad is the one interpreted by the militants to sanctify the notion of jihad, denoting jihad as synonymous with armed warfare.

This concept of Jihad has carried over by the jamaat to the current day and age. Despite its metamorphosis into a party with a political agenda, the Jamaat retains a strong Jihadi outlook. "Jamaat-e-Islami operates more than five hundred religious seminaries in Pakistan wherein significant numbers of foreign students also receive their education. There are several institutions wholly given to the education of foreigners of which the Maulana Maududi Institute in Lahore is the most important. There, selected students from all over the world are admitted. An important point with regard to this institution is that when tension was at its peak in Bosnia, Bosnian students were receiving their education in this madrasa and, when the military movement started in Chechnya, fifty per cent of the students there were from Chechnya … . … most of them leave before completing their academic year because they go to Jihadi training camps in Afghanistan and Kashmir during their vacations. However, all of them do not return from their vacations because they go on to destinations around the world. Some of these students join the al-Qaida network later."[47]

The Jamaat has repeatedly issued a vehement denial of any involvement with militant groups. Since the beginning of this century, the Jamaat has been an important actor in the Pakistani political scenario, albeit mostly in the opposition benches. However, it seems that it is at great pains to show its 'politically correct' face. In fact, since 2003, the establishment has tended to stay quiet about the Jamaat involvement, past or present, with militancy.

"The ISI, for the first time in its history, called a press conference on 12 March 2003 and categorically denied reports regarding links between Jamaat-e-Islami and al-Qaida. News regarding these links were published when an important al-Qaida member, Khalid Sheikh Mohammad, was arrested in the house of a member of jamat-e-Islami in Rawalpindi earlier in March that year. A similar incident had taken place earlier in Karachi also. According to other secret service sources, at least twelve members of al-Qaida were arrested

---

[47] Amir Rana, The seeds of Terrorism (London: New Millennium Press, 2005),209-10

either in the houses of Jamat members or else they had close links with them. The ISI official said in the press conference that Jamat did not have any links with al-Qaida even though some al-Qaida members might have had sympathies with them. He went on to argue that the whole organisation and its leadership could not be blamed on those grounds. It is certainly true that guilt cannot be inferred by association alone."[48] It is also certainly true, that in the highest echelons of power politics, deals are struck which at one unwritten stroke, wash away all past 'sins'. It may just be a euphemism, but researchers are rarely privy to the prerogatives of the high and mighty. We may not get to know the details of the 'deal' struck between the two entities mentioned above in the near future.

The greatest weakness of the Ikhwan model of political Islam is its dependence on a single charismatic leader, an Amir[49]; this precludes democratic participation in running the affairs of the organizational affairs. This can be seen by the obsession of radical Islam in choosing persons of only the purest belief, exemplary character, purity, virtues and qualifications etc. This is the attempt to install an Amir-ul-momineen, or leader of the believers; once in place the leader has considerable leeway in making his commands be accepted. This has allowed dictatorships to flourish, the Afghanistan of Hikmetyar and Mullah Omar, and now the Waziristan of Baitullah Mehsud. This is a consistent theme which should be remembered during any discourse on Taliban.

In Afghanistan, Afghani communists and Taliban as the pinnacle of Islamic extremism were the two dominant ideologies of the past decades. Both of them tried to impose radical change on a traditional social structure by a revolution from the top, which only resulted in an exponential increase in chaos. Their failure to account for the strong bonds of tribalism and ethnicity in the complex equation of social change, which they wanted to produce instantaneously, was a major reason for their failure.

The Taliban in Pakistan are attempting the same in an even more circumscribed area, where tribalism has been the main source of inspiration for centuries. It is debatable that they would succeed; the army operations in

---

[48] Ibid., 208-9.
[49] (Rashid, Pan Macmillan: 2001), 86.

the area, purportedly with American intelligence support, have made some headway recently[50]. However, the potential chaos created by this movement has less to do with the success of establishment of a Taliban/Al-Qaeda 'state-within-a-state', and more to do with the disorder created in the process of attempting to do so. The announcement of an umbrella body for Taliban in Pakistan has brought together a number of diverse guerilla groups together, and if the trend continues, it may very well become the penultimate headquarters of 'Radical Jihad International'.

The Taliban had initially set out as an Islamic reform movement, and before they had started indulging in cruelties, had succeeded in gaining some popularity as well. The Taliban were acting in the spirit of jihad when they attacked the rapacious warlords around them in Afghanistan. Yet, this degenerated in autocracy and ethnic killing in the name of the Taliban interpretation of jihad. This alienated the non-Pashtuns in Afghanistan, since the ethnic minorities saw them as using Islam as a cover to exterminate non-Pashtuns.

Their mode of thinking is indeed anti historical; history evolves and progresses; societal norms become reconceptualized around the nucleus of history, religious convictions in turn orienting themselves in the directions accorded them. Where there is relative stability and socio economic opportunities, religious convictions generally settle in to the mainstream. Certainly there are margins of aberration, but these are the fringes, not the mainstream. From the protestant Catholic divide to the war ravaged Afghanistan, this does seem to hold true. When there are gross disparities of social justice, extreme movements emerge and take hold, such as in Afghanistan and the currently developing situation in the northern areas of Pakistan. This maybe be somewhat of a generalization, as many extremists are demonstrably affluent ,such as the many so called 'Afghan Arabs' who have been in Afghanistan since long, the most notable of them being of course, Osama Bin laden himself. Many of the extremists would be western educated, or indeed have been born in the Western hemisphere. However, these are

---

[50] The situation has been developing over the past six months. For an overview of the latest situation in general, browse through the three most respected Pakistani news dailies during the days of July 15th to Aug 15th, 2008.The dailies are: Dawn, The news, Daily Times.

definitely lesser in numbers, though not in importance; the commonly seen media images of young, armed bearded men in Toyota pickups, are what constitute the substrate of terrorist indoctrination, aided by the catalyst of travesties of gross socio economic neglect.

The Taliban were a totally new religious phenomenon, devised piecemeal due to political exigencies. At the time they came into being, they fitted nowhere in the Islamic micro-cosmos; though it is debatable now that they have succeeded in creating a separate militant niche for themselves.. Nevertheless, even the radical Islamicists such as Ikhwan, considered the prototypes of Islamic terrorism, pale in comparison to the Taliban. They actively favoured and allowed women's education and participation in social life[51]. Indeed, a large part of their political support came from women, whom they organized in organizational structures. They attempted to develop rationale for Islamic systems for regulating economy, banking system, foreign relations and an equitable distributive social model. In this respect they were much more progressive than Taliban, even though they too suffered from the same weaknesses and limitations inherent in a polarized ideology; rejection of ideological and ethnic diversity which contributes to the evolution of a culture.

In examining the religious lineage of the New Taliban, it is worthwhile tracing the influence of Sufism on Afghanistan. Sufism was a moderating factor for Islam in Afghanistan; this being the trend of mystical Islam, which originated in Central Asia and Persia. Sufism is the mystical dimension of Islam. Classical scholars have defined it as "a science whose objective is the reparation of the heart and turning it away from all else but God"[52], or "a science through which one can know how to travel into the presence of the Divine, purify one's inner self from filth, and beautify it with a variety of praiseworthy traits."[53] The lexical root of Sufi is variously traced to the Arabic word for wool, referring to the simple cloaks the early Muslim ascetics wore, and to the Arabic word safa, meaning purity. The two lexicon meanings were

---

[51] (Rashid, Pan Macmillan: 2001), 86.
[52] Ahmed Zarruq, Zaineb Istrabadi, Hamza Yusuf Hanson - "The Principles of Sufism." Amal Press. 2008.
[53] The Autobiography (Fahrasa) of a Moroccan Soufi: Ahmad ibn 'Ajiba, translated from the Arabic by Jean-Louis Michon and David Streight, Fons Vitae, Louisville KY USA, 1999.

intertwined by al-Rudhabari: "The Sufi is the one who wears wool on top of purity".[54]

During the earlier Islamic period, a group of unmarried men living on their daily labour, and putting up on a mud platform called Suffa in the mosque, undertook the dissemination of Islamic teachings i.e. Quran and Ahadith to the converts and their families, without any remuneration. This small group of men known and respected for their piety and selfless service were called Ashaab-e-Suffa[55], and it is generally believed that Sufi cult was originally founded by them. Since they were religious visionaries and luminaries, they undertook exercises in spiritualism and philosophy in order to propagate Islam on behalf of the community as a collective religious obligation i.e. Farz-e-Kifaya. Sufism was essentially the result of Islam evolving in a more mystic direction. As the German scholar Annemarie Schimmel proposes, Sufism meant nothing but the "interiorization of Islam." It is from the Qur'an, constantly recited, meditated, and experienced, that Sufism proceeded, in its origin and its development.[56]

The Sufis never preached their Sufi beliefs known as Tasawwuf as a matter of general practice. They discriminated between ordinary moderate Muslims and those aspiring for a higher place in Islamic hierarchy. To the former, they taught the basic tenets of Islam in strictly conventional terms, and they initiated the latter in the mysteries inherent in mysticism and philosophy. The Sufi later founded four different Schools of Islamic mysticism, Qaderiyah, Chishtia, Suhrwardiya, and Naqshbandiyah, providing elasticity as against rigidity for attracting non-Muslims to convert. In the process, they borrowed practices alien to the Muslim faith. For example Qawwali, which is an admixture of instrumental and vocal music borrowed from Hinduism, was successfully used for attracting non-Muslims to the fold of Islam. As a reaction to this elasticity, formalism also raised its head in the movements like the one started by Abdul Wahab in the 19th century Arabian Desert. The Sufi way of life had always been under threat form the adherents of formalism, so

---

[54] Haddad, Gibril Fouad: Sufism in Islam LivingIslam.org: http://www.livingislam.org/k/si_e.html.
[55] Meaning literally, the followers of the Prophet.
[56] Massignon, Louis. Essai sur les origines du lexique technique de la mystique musulmane. Paris: Vrin, 1954. p. 104.

the evolution of Sufism and other mystical strains tended to be relegated to the back seat when puritanical movements took over.

There were two main Sufi orders in Afghanistan of Naqshbandiyah and Qaderiyah. These then provided a separate track of resistance to the soviets by their network of associations and alliances outside the Mujaheddin parties and ethnic groups. These were quite influential; The Mujaddedi family were leaders of the Naqshbandiyah their most prominent member being Sibghatullah Mujaddedi[57], the head of Jabha-i Najat Milli[58] Afghanistan set up in Peshawar, and later a president of Afghanistan in 1992, as chairman of the Jihad Council from 28 Apr to 28 Jun 1992.

The other important Sufi order was epitomized by Pir Sayed Ahmad Gilani[59]. He set up the Mahaz-e-Milli[60] in Peshawar. Even though Mujaddedi and Pir Gilani were leaders of mujahideen groups and received support initially from the ISI pipeline supplying finance, arms and ammunition to resistance groups, their views were too moderate to suit the pipeline managers. This was also due to the fact that they were moderate Muslims, and had their own conceptions about the conduct of warfare, which did not sit well with Jihad organizing nexus of CIA/ISI, who demanded aggressive offensives. The CIA–ISI nexus preferred the ultra Islamist viewpoints of Hikmetyar and later the Taliban; and also initially, the effective blitzkrieg techniques employed by Ahmed Shah Masud. Thus, the Taliban did not incorporate in their ideology the moderating influence of Sufism, which tends to be moderate in outlook.

As regards FATA, is would be an illuminating exercise to look into their contemporary religious mindset; this is not possible without considering the tribal structures in FATA in their contextual paradigms.

North Waziristan is home to about 375,000 people, mostly belonging to the Wazir and Dawar tribes. Many militant tribal leaders have become legendary figures in the area. This was a largely reactionary area even from the independence of Pakistan since 1947, even though many tribesmen are

---

[57] (Rashid, Pan Macmillan: 2001), 84.
[58] National Liberation Front of Afghanistan.
[59] (Rashid, Pan Macmillan: 2001), 85.
[60] National Islamic Front of Afghanistan

enrolled in the Pakistan army. The strong Pashtun identity of these people has meant that they relate more with Afghanistan than Pakistan.

South Waziristan is the largest tribal agency in size, having a population of about 425,000 tribesmen from Mehsud and Wazir tribes. Both tribes are renowned as formidable warriors, a tradition they keep alive by their frequently erupting blood feuds. According to historian Sir Olaf Caroe, the Mehsud tribe would never consider submitting to a foreign power that has entered their land. Nek Mohammad was a legendary militant leader from this agency, who was succeeded by Baitullah Mehsud .I shall dwell upon both these areas in greater detail later.

Bajaur's prominent tribes are Tarkani and Utman Khel. The JUI has tremendous influence in this area. Over the years, there have been some unconfirmed media reports about the possibility of Osama bin Laden hiding in the area. This area is currently the main area of army operations against militancy; heavy fighting has been reported, with 300,000 residents being forced to evacuate the area due to heavy artillery shelling. This area too, will merit much greater interest when I dwell upon the operational side of the new Taliban forces.

In Khyber agency, the main inhabitants are the Afridis and the Shinwaris. Afridis have been known in history as good fighters and respectful to Sufis (mystics) and their shrines, which intellectually aligns them with Barelvi Sunnis, the antidote of conservative and pro-Taliban Deobandi groups. The Shinwaris, who are mostly businessmen, mostly reside in the Ningrahar province of Afghanistan. Khyber Agency has been prone to develop into a prime trouble spot, known for hosting illegal radio stations supporting religious extremism and encouraging pro-Taliban activities (Dawn, December 2, 2004; Dawn, December 19, 2005).

The influence of relatively high educational rates for Orakzai Agency has not stopped its tribes from falling under the thralls of Talibanisation. They are amongst the most conservative of the tribals, being amongst the first to ban NGO's from operating in the area, declaring them anti-Islamic. The possession of televisions was declared a punishable crime under the influence of the local Taliban. Most of the state run educational institutions have been shut down by the local Taliban.

Mohmands, residing in Mohmand agency, are natural guerrilla fighters. A characteristic hallmark of these people is that they are particularly reverent to their religious leaders, to the extent of fighting their wars under leadership of local clerics.

The Kurram agency is mostly inhabited mainly by the Shiite Bangash tribe, which makes it anti-Taliban by default. The other tribe, Turi (Turkic origin), has also constantly been at loggerheads with pro-Taliban, Deobandi elements in the neighboring areas.

Thus, a cursory look at some of the FATA areas reveals a more conservative and inward looking society than Afghanistan considered as a whole; thus it seems that these areas (with few exceptions) are viable religious substrate for militant fundamentalism to take hold. It is not surprising that the emergence of Pakistan's Taliban has occurred in these areas.

The Taliban are poles apart from the tolerant Sufis, and are also far removed from the traditionalists who, at least, tend to rely on interpretative discourse to justify their existence. Strictly speaking, they are neither radical Islamicists inspired by the Ikhwan, nor mystical Sufis, nor traditionalists. It can be said that all three systems of thinking had failed Afghanistan between 1979 and 1994.Thus, the Taliban neatly filled in the vacuum.

Comprehension of the religious milieu of the Taliban, demands a close look at the politico-religious evolution of Islam in Afghanistan. Many commentators, particularly western ones, err in assuming that the Taliban's religious ideology was a distillation of the Islamic thought process in Afghanistan; history shows otherwise.

Adherence to Islamic ritualism is inbred in the lifestyle of the Afghanis and the Pakistani tribals, regardless of whether they really are religious or not. The panoply of adherents includes ex-King Zahir Shah, communist pro Russian ministers, and Mujahideen warriors. That is the point, however, when the analogy breaks down; Islam in Afghanistan has historically been extremely tolerant, and not at all the 'push it down your throat' type[61]. Minorities such as Sikhs, Hindus and Jews had enjoyed minimal persecution in Afghanistan; in fact they were quite wealthy and controlled the money

---

[61] (Rashid, Pan Macmillan: 2001), 82.

markets. Even the Afghan mullah was a laissez faire variety of preacher who would admonish people for not coming to prayers regularly, but would rarely preach sectarianism and politics. The year 1992 saw a watershed; this year, not coincidentally, corresponds to the Taliban gaining strength in Afghanistan.

After 1992 the brutal civil war created irreconcilable schisms within Islamic sects and ethnic groups, setting the stage for the contemporary intolerant Afghanistan. Masud's massacre of the Hazaras in Kabul in 1995, the Hazaras' massacre of the Taliban in Mazar in 1997, and the Taliban massacres of Hazaras and Uzbeks in 1998 mark brutal 'Islamocide' perpetrated by Muslims in the name of their indigenous breed of ideology[62]. This was a novel phenomenon in Afghanistan's history, creating the present religious divides. Minority groups all but fled the country, since the ethnocide committed above, coupled with the Taliban's deliberate anti-Shia programme, transformed the fiercely independent tribalism of the Afghanis into a militant fundamentalism.

Eighty per cent of people in Afghanistan belong to the Sunni Hanafi sect, which is by large considered the most liberal amongst the four Sunni schools of thought.[63] The minority strains were the Shia Islam of the Hazaras in the Hazarajat, the beliefs of scattered Pashtun tribes, Tajiks and Heratis, and the Ismaelis, the followers of the Agha Khan.

Even though there is no separation of politics from religion, the Sunni Hanafi creed prevalent in Afghanistan for ages admirably suited the loose Afghan confederation politics, since it was quite flexible. Tribalism being the preferred state of government, state interference was kept to a minimum. The Pashtun village mullahs were the centre of village and social life, and Jirga the preferred adjudicative body.

More formal education was done in small madrassahs where Students or Talibs studied the basic tenets of religious education. Herat was a central nucleus of learning in Afghanistan society, though from seventeenth century onwards, Talibs aspiring to a higher level of religious learning traveled to Central Asia, Egypt and India to study at more renowned madrassahs.

Islam was also embedded in the political structure in Afghanistan because Sharia law governed the legal processes late as 1925; a civil legal code was

---

[62] Ibid.,83
[63] Ibid.

introduced as a symbiont to enable both systems to grow together. A Sharia Faculty was set up in Kabul University in 1946[64]. A protégé of this eclectic mix was Mohammed Musa Shafiq, the populist last Prime Minister under the monarchy, who was later executed by the communists. Shafiq combined all tiers of education; a madrassah education, the Sharia Faculty in Kabul, followed by a degree from Columbia University in New York.

As the emphasis was more on tribalism than religious inclinations, the more traditional tribal-based parties were thus preferred by the afghan ulema as opposed to radical one. At the onset of Jihad, most joined Harakat Inquilabi-Islami headed by Maulana Mohammed Nabi Mohammedi and Hizb-e-Islami led by Maulvi Younis Khalis[65]. Both men were maulvis who had studied for a time at the Haqqania madrassah in Pakistan and then established their own madrassahs inside Afghanistan. After the Soviet invasion they set up organizations which were decentralized, non-ideological and non-hierarchical, but they rapidly lost out as the CIA–ISI arms pipeline supported the more radical Islamic parties.

Before the Taliban, Islamic extremism never really managed to gain a foothold in Afghanistan. The Wahabi sect for example, permeated from central Asia and India, but was a movement of inconsequential importance before the ascendancy of the Taliban. However, the Saudis preferred the Wahabi warlords to give their money to; an early export was Abdul Rasul Sayyaf, who set up a Wahabi party, the Ittehad-e-Islami, Islamic Unity, in Peshawar. He can be characterized as the archetypical conservative, "anti-West," "anti-American" and hard line Islamic fundamentalist. He was a scion of Al-Azhar University in Cairo, Egypt, and a member of the afghani group Akhwan-ul-Muslimeen (Muslim Brotherhood) founded in 1969 by Gulbeddin Hikmetyar and Dr. Syed Burhanuddin Rabbani. This was defined by some as just a chapter of the Muslim Brotherhood in Egypt.

Sayyaf cultivated a close relationship with Osama bin Laden, establishing a network of training camps, bunkers and emplacements in the Jalalabad area with mutual collaboration, which were later utilized by Al-Qaeda personnel. ("Former bin Laden mentor warns the West," Telegraph 03/12/2001) The

---

[64] Ibid., 84.
[65] Ibid.

Wahabi strain of puritanical thought was further distilled in the thought process of Afghans; this strain is known by the name of Salafism. Ordinary Afghans however considered this movement with disdain, because of their inbred distrust of anything foreign, whom they traditionally view with great suspicion. Even Bin Laden, when he joined the afghan jihad, was considered as an 'outsider'; however, in war, finances tend to get depleted at an alarming rate; freely available money is welcome, which eventually enabled him to win a small Pashtun following. However, afghan Arabs continued to be treated as outsiders by Afghanis, who were not above murdering them at times out of disdain for their 'arrogance' and what the afghans saw as 'holier than thou' attitudes.

Pakistan had under its tutelage commanders of the caliber of Hikmetyar and Masud since 1975, before the soviet invasion, both being forced to flee Afghanistan due to failed uprisings against President Mohammed Daud .They had been cultivated by the ISI for the purpose whey they were admirably suited to, when the invasion of Afghanistan began. President Zia ul Haq was thus the supporter of both these groups. Masud however was a commander with a mind of his own (and he was also more secular minded); this caused him to drift away from the Pakistani government eventually, leaving Hikmetyar as the sole recipient of the cash flowing in. Not coincidentally, Hikmetyar was also the most radically minded of all mujahideen. The continued Pakistani support to him sometimes flew in the face of facts on ground; he was not very well accepted in Kabul, Masud having greater credibility in the eyes of ordinary Afghans.

It can thus be seen that the ideological sanction for the Taliban was basically imposed by external sources, the most militant ideologies competing for the cash and ammunition. Pakistan was the main indoctrination base for the Taliban ideology; it follows naturally that the 'New' Taliban have imbibed the philosophy from the infrastructure of madrassahs remaining largely intact, despite ineffectual efforts by the Pakistani authorities to regulate their curriculum. It seems that the madrassahs in the FATA area have not only largely remained intact, they have in fact prospered. Having filled in the contextual parameters, it is time to introduce the predominant influence on the thought process of the old and new Taliban.

The Taliban represented nobody but themselves and they recognized no Islam except their own. But they did have an ideological base – an extreme right leaning improvised form of Deobandism, which was being preached by Pakistani Islamic parties in Afghan refugee camps in Pakistan. The Deobandis, a branch of Sunni Hanafi Islam has had a history in Afghanistan, but the Taliban's interpretation of the creed has no parallel anywhere in the Muslim world.

The Deobandis arose as a religious revivalism movement designed to arrest the deterioration of Muslims in post mutiny (1857) British India; its main ideologues were Mohammed Qasim Nanautawi (1833-77) and Rashid Ahmed Gangohi (1829–1905), who founded the first madrassah in Deoband near New Delhi. The Deobandis original agenda was to train a new generation of learned Muslims involved in a revivalist Islamic movement based on intellectual learning and spiritual experience[66]. The interpretation of sharia is aimed to harmonize it with the current realities of the mundane as well as the spiritual world. Even though they were revivalist, they had an intrinsically orthodox outlook; a restrictive view of the role of women, an open condemnation of Shiites and vehement opposition to a hierarchical Islamic state was their forte. The Taliban were to take these beliefs to an extreme which the original Deobandis would never have recognized. The Deobandis had set up network of madrassahs all over India, and Afghan students, after the decline of Herat as an intellectual centre, began to arrive in large numbers to get educated in a better manner in these more reputable madrassahs. By 1967, there were 9,000 Deobandi madrassahs across South Asia[67].

A few Deobandi madrassahs were established by the Afghan state, but they were not hugely popular even in the Pashtun belt. The Deobandi school of thought gained great impetus during the Afghan jihad, since much of the teaching in madrassahs was carried out by organizations, particularly JUI.

It is relevant to point out that the current face of Deobandi learning has been seen as a threat by the west, even in local home bred clerics of the domestic order. For instance, in the UK, a Times policy report has mentioned

---

[66] Jm Butt, Controversy: Targeting madrassas to curb extremism?, Daily Times August 17, 2008.
[67] (Rashid, Pan Macmillan: 2001), 88.

that the Deobandi movement "supports armed jihad and preaches contempt for Jews, Christians and Hindus, is in line to become the spiritual leader of the Deobandi sect in Britain. The ultra-conservative movement, which gave birth to the Taleban in Afghanistan, now runs more than 600 of Britain's 1,350 mosques."[68] A commentator on religious radicalism in Pakistan, where Deobandis wield significant political influence, told The Times that "blind ignorance" on the part of the Government in Britain had allowed the Deobandis to become the dominant voice of Islam in Britain's mosques.

Khaled Ahmed said: "The UK has been ruined by the puritanism of the Deobandis. You've allowed the takeover of the mosques. You can't run multiculturalism like that, because that's a way of destroying yourself. In Britain, the Deobandi message has become even more extreme than it is in Pakistan. It's mind-boggling."[69]

Deobandi school of thought was primarily revivalist and intellectual, though it did have puritanical sanction behind it. Though there are both sides of the issue[70], it would be closing our eyes to the reality if we do not recognize Political Islam as an entity, albeit as one opposed to the peaceful message of Islam as a religion. This topic is beyond the scope of this study, but I believe it merits further research.

After Pakistan 's creation in 1947, two watersheds in Deobandi history occurred; madrassahs began to spring up at a greater rate, and the Deobandis set up the Jamiat Ulema Islam(JUI), an evangelical movement. In 1962 it transformed into a political party under the leadership of Maulana Ghulam Ghaus Hazarvi in NWFP. There were soon schisms afterwards, and the rifts produced a distinct Pashtun dominated version of the party under the popular Maulana Mufti Mehmood(1919-80), characterized by a strong anti-American, anti-imperialist stance. The JUI competed for power with the Jamaat-e-Islami, and the relationship has varied from cool hostility to wary partnerships over the years. Fazlur Rehman, Mufti Mehmood's son, took over from him; if any

---

[68] Andrew Norfolk, Hardline takeover of British mosques, The Times, September 7, 2007. http://www.timesonline.co.uk/tol/comment/faith/article2402973.ece.
[69] Ibid.
[70] For a criticism of this report see: http://www.guardian.co.uk/commentisfree/2007/sep/07/atoxicmixoffactandnonsense

one can lay claim to be considered the spiritual mentor of Taliban, it is him, though he is now at pains to deny it.

It should be of interest to the reader that Taliban, being trained mostly in the traditions of Pashtunwali, and lacking in the ideological and academic perspective of the Deobandi School, were far behind relative accomplishment which JUI had to impart at a later stage during the General Zia regime, because initially the JUI were not given official patronage. With the gradual collapse of the academic system and denial of educational facilities to the poor and the needy, the people living below subsistence level in Pakistan started acquiring religious education; because after all it had the semblance of education simultaneously affording food, shelter, monetary benefits for the students and their families, and necessary military training in order to prepare combatants/ militants to fight for the cause of Islam. General Zia started heavy funding for these madrassahs; around 900 in number in 1971, which quickly shot up to 28,000 in 1988; and according to a source, 25,000 unregistered institutions existed at the end of Zia era. According to another estimate, madrassahs in Pakistan had sharply grown from 1,745 in 1979 to around 15,000 in the year 2000. In Punjab Province alone, the number of the registered students in madrassahs was 2, 19,000.[71] According to another credible source, in 1997, there were 2,512 madrassahs and 218,939 students in eight districts (Lahore, Gujranwala, Rawalpindi, Faisalabad, Sargodha, Multan, D.G. Khan, and Bahawalpur) of the Punjab province. 972 madrassahs belonged to the Deobandi sect with 100,558 students, 1,216 to the Barelvi sect with 95,190 students, 174 to the Ahle-Hadith sect with 18,880 students and 100 to Ahle Tashi sect with 4,281 students registered in them.[72]

Even though they were sidelined pertaining to funding by the ISI earlier, JUI availed the opportunity offered by General (Retired) Farhatullah Babar during the tenure of Benazir Bhutto in 1993, when the above referred General was keen to introduce this political party to the corridors of power in order to assign it a significant role amongst Pashtuns in NWFP and Afghanistan.

---

[71] Suba Chandran, 'Madrassas in Pakistan: A Brief Overview', Institute of Peace and Conflict Studies, 25 January 2000. http://www.ipcs.org/index.jsp.
[72] Lt. Gen. (R) Kamal Matinuddin, The Taliban Phenomenon; Oxford University Press, 1999.Also see Kamal Matinuddin, Power Struggle in Hindukush; Wajidalis, Lahore, 1991.

Simultaneously, JUI was aspiring for a peeping window to Central Asian States and their Pashtuns, Kirghis, and Uzbek residents, with the ultimate objective of reaching Chechnya and Bosnia through their access to Europe and United States. The opportunity arose quicker than they had expected; when Maulana Fazal-ur-Rehman headed the special committee for foreign affairs. Now they were all powerful inasmuch as the services of Inter-Services Intelligence (ISI) with immense financial resources were placed at their disposal. Gradually Saudi Arabia also funneled financial aid to JUI and its religious educational madrassahs, performing the dual role of creating sympathizers for the Wahabism on one hand and preparing militants for the Soviet-Afghan armed on the other.

Fazlur Rehman's credentials in the creation of the Afghan Taliban are so well established, that I need not dwell at length upon it. We are currently more focused on analyzing whether he is a source of ideological sanction for the New Taliban as well.

"Very few people know that during the Taliban regime's period of power, only Maulana Samiul Haq and Maulana Fazlur Rehman had authority to issue passes to Arab and other foreign mujahideen to join the Taliban forces. It was essential to have a card signed by Maulana Samiul Haq for entering Afghanistan from the Frontier Province and a card signed by Maulana Fazlur Rehman for entering Afghanistan from Baluchistan...... Only those with a card could receive training in the camps. The foreigners were supposed to have these cards for security purposes but this condition did not apply to Pakistanis and the Pushtons[73] who could join any jihadi organisation to go to Afghanistan to receive their training."[74]

There are also report on record that the Maulana was an important conduit between the ISI and the Taliban in Kabul. When ISI got news of an imminent

---

[73] It is common to find variations in the spellings used by different authors; the lexical meanings sometimes have no counterpart in the English language, and varying authors use different spellings for the same words. The word 'Pashtons' used here is a case in point; I prefer the more formal spelling of 'Pashtuns' which corresponds (according to my personal preference) with the Pashto sound of the word. Different authors have different preferences. Some would use 'madrassa' instead of my preference for 'madrassha'. None are incorrect, since they represent lexical preferences. However, when quoting an author, I naturally have to retain the syntax used by him.

[74] (Rana,2005), 200-1.

attack upon Taliban by Ahmed Shah Masud, the Maulana was dispatched to Afghanistan in all haste to relay this information to the Taliban.[75] The Americans reportedly got wind of this, and reportedly stepped up efforts to contain the Maulana. As with all such matters, the exact details are shrouded in secrecy.

The Maulana has been a sitting member of the National assembly in Pakistan for some time now. He was a pivotal part of the alliance of religious parties going under the umbrella body of Muttahida Majlis-e-Amal. As with the Jamaat mentioned above, he seems to have adopted a 'politically correct' stance:-

"I think I managed to overcome this image during my 10-day visit to India. By the end of the visit, the media was saying that I was more of a politician than a Maulana. They were also writing that I was a soft-liner rather than a hard-liner. ... I kept telling the Indians that we surely did back the Taliban because they were a continuation of the Afghan mujahideen who fought against the Soviet occupation troops in Afghanistan. We considered the Taliban freedom fighters in the same way as the Palestinians and Chechens but at the end of the day they were Afghans and we are Pakistanis and we operate in different situations."[76]

This however does not seem to sit too well with the situation on the ground. "There is a persistent allegation against Maulana Fazlur Rahman's Jamiat Ulema-e-Islam that it is still helping to get the Taliban reorganized in Chaman and Quetta and the madrasas are providing a safe haven for them in the frontier areas. The JUI leadership, however, denies this allegation. One Jamiat Ulema-e-Islam leader, Hafiz Hussain Ahmad, said that the JUI was not a properly organised political entity. He said that it had its own individual policies, madrasas and mosques in the cities and it was not mandatory that these policies conformed with any central policy."[77] It may be worthwhile to point out that Chaman[78] in Baluchistan is a border town with Afghanistan. It is undoubtedly a rallying point for many of the Taliban that fled Afghanistan;

---

[75] Nidai Millat, 19 august 1999.
[76] The News,3 August,2003.
[77] (Rana,2005), 207.
[78] For a detailed discussion about this phenomenon, read article by author "The new taliban-1:Emergence"

much of the reorganization of the new Taliban would purportedly have been done there. The JUI driven madrassas were fed with funds not only to teach Afghan refugee youngsters, but a considerable number of Pakistani homes began sending their wards to schools and madrassas run by Islamic parties. Families in the rural areas did not have money to afford education for their children. Many families on or below the poverty line sent their children to madrassas. Some Islamists had an incentive scheme of a sort; if a family provided one of its sons for Jihad, not only all the other siblings received a free education, but the family was also granted a subsistence allowance. The state was unable to meet this challenge in a climate of diminishing investment in public education because funds were pre empted by defense and elitist expenditures. Thus, the politic-religious organizations like JUI made great use of this vacuum in socio-economic provision by the state to increase the number of their adherents.

The JUII exercises a great following in the North and South Waziristan Agencies, Hangu, Bannu and the peripheries of Dera Ismail Khan, which stand out as economically backward areas and where conservative traditions have a hold on society. The JUI-F has a deep influence in these areas by virtue of combining Pashtunwali with religious ideologies. On December 13, 1999, one person was publicly executed for killing his cousin after being sentenced to death by the local Taliban judicial court. This was the first such execution by a Pakistani Taliban group and the local Taliban leader, Mullah Rahim, termed it as the first step towards the enforcement of the Sharia.[79]

As with any organization that is doing extraordinarily well, factions had to emerge in JUI because of this financial booty, as well as for influence amongst the Afghans Mujahideen. The above referred opportunity soon emerged when Maulana Sami-ul-Haq made use of the religious institution Dar-ul-Uloom Haqqania founded by his father Abdul Aziz in 1947, who studied and worked as a teacher in Dar-ul-Uloom Deoband. This institution exists on a fairly vast piece of land in Akora Khattak on Islamabad-Peshawar Highway with boarding & lodging facilities for 1500 students, a High School for 1,000 students and buildings for 12 elementary madrassahs. It offered an eight years

---

[79] Ismail Khan, 'The Talibanisation of Pakistan', Newsline, Karachi, January 1999, p. 44.

course for Masters Degrees, and additional two years for Doctorate. Accommodation and tuition being free, this institution attracted a lot of students after the collapse of Pakistan's national academic system; when people in general and particularly those living below subsistence level couldn't afford to pay for their studies. It shouldn't, therefore, surprise anyone that eight of their trainee Talibans were serving as Cabinet Ministers in Kabul, whereas about twelve of their graduates were working as Governors on behalf of the Taliban Government in Afghanistan[80]. These madrassahs are reaping the harvest because of the defective planning in Pakistan, making education more or less inaccessible for a common man; resulting almost in a total collapse of the existing educational system in the country. In the absence of state control, the mushroom growth of these madrassahs are creating terrorism through a process of mass production whose activities are difficult to be checked; especially in view of the sympathies of the local population for them.

Samiul Haq has always professed deep respect for Mullah Omar. According to him, he went to see Mullah Omar in Qandhar in 1996 when he was elected Amir-ul-Momineen despite not occupying a very high station or high pedigree, but a simple pious man; who could deliver the goods in compliance of the Islamic injunctions. Hence he was immensely qualified for this job. "I met Omar for the first time when I went to Kandahar in 1996 and I was proud that he was chosen as Amir-ul Momineen. He has no money, tribe or pedigree but he is revered above all others and so Allah chose him to be their leader. According to Islam the man who can bring peace can be elected the Amir. When the Islamic revolution comes to Pakistan it will not be led by the old defunct leaders like me, but by a similiar unknown man who will arise from the masses."[81]

Sami-ul-Haq's madrassahs have been a source of strength for Taliban,[82] to be relied upon in times of emergency. He remains at the beck and call of Mullah Omar and sent his entire student's body to Afghanistan in Mazar Sharif after closing down his madrassahs for about a month.

---

[80] (Rashid, Pan Macmillan: 2001), 90.
[81] Ibid., 91.
[82] Shafqat Jan, the Cantonment of Islam, The Nation, August 29, 1999.

"It is well known that Jamia Haqqania and the madrasa at Akora Khatak and had been in contact with the Taliban and al-Qaida even though Maulana Samiul Haq denies this. He said (25 May 2003) that he has been receiving information regarding the Taliban and that Mullah Omar and Osama bin Laden are not only well but are also guiding their mujahideen in the jihad against America. There is information regarding some other members of Maulana Samiul Haq's group that establishes their links with the Taliban and al-Qaida. When Maulana Yusuf Shah, the General Secretary of JUI (Sami-ul-Haq group) was asked whether some Al-Qaida mujahideen were, according to some reports, taking refuge in the madrasa of Maulana Abdul Aziz Hashmi, he openly wondered if there was anything wrong in that. He said: "It is not a crime for us to provide refuge or to help mujahideen."[83]

Another splinter faction of JUI was the madrassah of Maulana Yusuf Binori, at Binor near Karachi. Its name is Jamiut-Uloomi-Islamiyya, run with the financial assistance of forty five Muslim countries. A number of Taliban leaders with important portfolios in Taliban Afghanistan have studied here. This madrassah had at one time 8,000 students on its roll, and has sent 600 of them to Afghanistan to help Taliban on their appeal for help and assistance during armed skirmishes. Many of the two million Afghan refugees settled in Baluchistan or Karachi were influenced by the Binori variant of madrassah education. In 1997 Karachi saw the Taliban from this madrassah rampage on a rather wide scale, and this cosmopolitan town was exposed to Taliban style terrorism for the first time ever. It is pertinent to mention that Karachi is currently facing a grave threat from Talibanisation of its society, much of which can be ascribed to the students from this seminary. Thus, almost all the children born in camps or in villages and cities of Pakistan, especially in NWFP, tribal areas of Pakistan, Karachi or Baluchistan were provided grounding in Islamic education of the Deobandi School, primarily by the above mentioned groups.

An organization worth mentioning here for their linkages with JUI is the Sipah-e-Sahaba Pakistan (SSP). They are responsible for killing members of Shia community and Shia elites in almost all walks of life. Their targets were

---

[83] (Rana, 2005), 208.

generally the eminent Physicians/Surgeons, Engineers, lawyers, businessmen, religious scholars, Government Officers in top hierarchy, and Litterateurs (particularly poets). They specialized in hit & run techniques, and were rarely apprehended after the commitment of a crime i.e. murder. They set up a base in Kabul in 1998 in order to get sanctuary from Taliban; where they were imparted military training in Khost Military camp run jointly by the Taliban and Bin Laden. They have since been fighting along side with Taliban ever since, and are responsible for multitudinous killings on sectarian basis both inside and outside Pakistan. When their activities went unchecked for a fairly long time causing sizeable damage to citizenry on both sides of the border, US hit their camp with a cruise missile in 1998.

Taliban made a generous offer to Sipah-e-Sahaba Pakistan, (SSP) for handing over the control of camps run by Hikmetyar, as training camps for Mujahideen of non-Afghan origin. Military Training camp at Badar-al-Khalil near Khost on Pakistan-Afghanistan border was handed over to Harkat-ul-Ansar fighting under the command of Fazal-ur-Rehman Khalil. This group was again an offshoot of JUI; which was gradually expanding its sphere of influence for being visualized as a power to be reckoned with by the neighboring Muslim States. This group, which was basically a faction of JUI, was known for its extreme Islamic radicalism, sending its volunteers to fight in Chechnya, Bosnia, Kashmir, and Afghanistan.

It might incidentally be mentioned here, that JUI represents a common linkage of faith amongst Deobandis, discarding federalism, tribalism, and the concept of a tribal chief by Pashtuns. This has become a strong religious bond; reinforcing confidence and credibility proving extraordinarily helpful in the struggle they are undergoing. Another strong bond between JUI and SSP is their hostility towards Shias and the Shia State of Iran. Hence Deobandi ideology is gaining ground amongst tribals on either side of the border due to this common sectarian heritage. Besides, the origin of these new Deobandi brothers (i.e. the afghan and Pakistani Taliban) is from the Durrani Pashtun tribe located in Qandhar on Afghanistan side and in Chaman on this side of the border. It is, therefore, not surprising that Deobandis living in Pakistan are aspiring for a Taliban type of revolution in Pakistan. However, the brand of

Deobandism they preach is entirely their own invention, utterly bereft of the scholarly pursuit by Deobandi scholars during the past.

CONCLUSION

Inside Pakistan, there is present a conjunction of politico-religious forces which undoubtedly have strong have links with the Afghan Taliban, and have been emboldened by their successes against soviets and the afghan warlords. They consider the allied campaign as a challenge; this is the beginning of a new jihad, but the Taliban needed a new base to consolidate their organizational strength. They have found that strength in the tribal areas of Pakistan. The American and allied presence in Afghanistan have robbed them of many of their previously held strongholds; this can be countered by the establishment of a Taliban-style insurgency in Pakistan. Some of the hardliner aspersions are decidedly ambitious, favoring a Taliban style take-over in Pakistan.[84] As mentioned above, even if this does not seem an imminent reality, the Taliban in Pakistan have the potential to cause grave disorder and chaos on an already overburdened economy and faltering political processes. An unstable Pakistan is a geopolitical disaster for the region, and the Global War on Terror. I strongly endorse Nasim Zehra's views regarding the current situation: "Pakistan will play "as clean as the world around it." This is the reality. Take it or leave it. There is no "going it alone" on the victory dais for any of Pakistan's neighbours. No matter what anyone's GDP may be or their nuclear arsenal may boast of, we are in this mess together. The way out lies only in working together; divided we all drown. That is the message of the fast spreading militancy which, with every new subversion move that anyone from

---

[84] The Cost of Defending Taliban', Prof. Khalid Mahmood, The News, 17 December, 1998.

the neighborhood induct against the other, gets more and more deadly and uncontrollable. The region will unravel if the governments in the area and those involved outsiders like Washington do not make it a common cause to jointly work to address the causes of growing militancy. The answer lies in a regional solution. We need to give up historical suspicions, the current score-settling and status hang-ups to work to create a more trusting environment within which a more cooperative security approach is evolved."[85]

---

[85] Nasim Zehra" Militancy and the regional challenge", The News Newspaper, August 06, 2008. http://thenews.jang.com.pk/daily_detail.asp?id=128453

INDEX

9

9/11, 2, 3, 12

A

Abdullah, 14, 18
academic, 14, 34, 47, 51
access, 2, 10, 21, 48
adaptation, 7
administration, 20
administrative, 7
administrators, 6, 7
adult, 8
Afghanistan, vii, 2, 3, 5, 6, 11, 15, 16, 17, 18, 19, 20, 21, 22, 23, 24, 25, 29, 34, 35, 36, 37, 39, 40, 41, 42, 43, 44, 45, 46, 47, 48, 49, 51, 52, 53, 55
age, 33, 34
agents, 7, 8
aggression, 18, 26
agriculture, 9, 10
aid, vii, 14, 48
aircraft, 15
Al Qaeda, 26
alien, 2, 38
aliens, 21
Allah, 30, 31, 32, 51
allies, 19, 26
alternative, 10
analysts, 15
anti-American, 19, 43, 46
Arab world, 25
Arabia, 48
Arabs, 16, 36, 44
Armed Forces, 10
Army, 20
arrest, 45
Asia, 6, 22, 37, 42, 43, 45
Asian, 6, 48
assessment, 9
associations, 39
attacks, 20
attitudes, 31, 44
authoritarianism, 2
authority, 7, 20, 48

B

Baluchistan, 5, 18, 22, 23, 24, 48, 49, 52
Bangladesh, 16
banking, 37
barrier, 12
beliefs, 38, 42, 45
benchmark, 4
benefits, 47
Bin Laden, 29, 44, 53
birth, 15, 46
black, 23

blood, 6, 40
bonds, 35
border crossing, 16
Bosnia, 34, 48, 53
Bosnian, 34
boys, 17, 19
Britain, 46
British, 5, 6, 7, 8, 10, 11, 22, 45, 46
brothers, 26, 53
buildings, 50
Bush administration, 20
business, 9, 18

C

caliber, 44
capital, 13, 15, 19
cash flow, 44
cassettes, 25
catalyst, 37
Catholic, 36
Central Asia, 6, 37, 42, 48
centralized, 32
chaos, 29, 35, 36, 55
chaotic, 29
Chechnya, 34, 48, 53
children, 13, 50, 52
China, 26
Christians, 46
CIA, 2, 3, 39, 43
citizens, 5, 10
civil society, 4
civil war, 42
clothing, 19
co-existence, 1
cognitive, 12, 13
collaboration, 43
colonial, 6, 7, 31
combat, 18
community, 33, 38, 52
complexity, 1, 26
compliance, 51
comprehension, vii, 3, 14
computer, 19
confidence, 53
conflict, 23

consolidation, 19
constitutional, 30
consumer goods, 9
contempt, 5, 46
continuity, 11
control, 6, 7, 17, 19, 51, 53
controlled, 41
corridors, 47
corruption, 8
courts, 8
covering, 23
credentials, 31, 48
credibility, 44, 53
creep, 14
crime, 40, 52, 53
crimes, 7
criticism, 26, 46
crossing over, 21
cultural, 12, 26
culture, 12, 37
currency, 25
curriculum, 44

D

dailies, 36
danger, 3
death, 50
decentralized, 43
decision making, 7
defense, 16, 50
defenses, 7
degree, 43
delivery, 16
demand, 14
democracy, 8
denial, 34, 47
deprivation, 12
disaster, 55
discourse, 2, 4, 22, 31, 35, 41
disorder, 36, 55
distillation, 41
diversity, 37
doctor, 10
donations, 23
drinking, 10

drinking water, 10
drug trafficking, 9
dualism, 4
duality, 5

E

early warning, 14
economic, 2, 9, 12, 13, 16, 26, 36, 50
economic development, 2
economic indicator, 9
economy, 9, 37, 55
education, 10, 12, 13, 18, 22, 34, 37, 42, 43, 47, 50, 51, 52
educational institutions, 12, 40
educational system, 51
Egypt, 30, 42, 43
Egyptian, 15
elasticity, 38
elders, 8, 10
employment, 10
empowered, 7
engineering, 15
English, 19, 48
environment, 56
equilibrium, 4
equipment, 23
ethnic diversity, 37
ethnic groups, 39, 42
ethnicity, 14, 25, 31, 35
Europe, 48
evidence, 21
evolution, vii, 3, 5, 14, 30, 37, 39, 41
exclusion, 12
execution, 50
exercise, 7, 39
expenditures, 50
expert, 19
exploitation, 12
explosive, 25
exponential, 35
extremism, 1, 2, 35, 40, 43, 45
eyes, 2, 7, 17, 44, 46

F

failure, 4, 35
faith, 4, 26, 31, 38, 46, 53
family, 8, 39, 50
farm, 19
Fata, 2, 4
fear, 20
federal government, 8
federalism, 53
Federally administered Tribal Areas, 2
feelings, 12, 26
females, 10
fighters, 8, 15, 20, 23, 40, 41, 49
finance, 39
financial aid, 48
financial resources, 48
financial support, 26
fines, 7
flood, 23
food, 11, 22, 47
foreign affairs, 48
foreigners, 12, 34, 48
formal education, 42
franchise, 8
freedom, 49
freedom fighter, 49
fuel, 23
funding, 47
funds, 23, 50

G

GDP, 16, 55
genealogy, 6
generalization, 36
generation, 7, 23, 45
Genghis Khan, 6
genocide, 25
Global War on Terror (GWOT), 1, 55
God, 24, 31, 33, 37
government, iv, 3, 6, 8, 14, 15, 17, 18, 21, 23, 25, 31, 42, 44, 56
grants, 6
gravity, vii, 26

grounding, 52
groups, 1, 2, 15, 17, 19, 23, 24, 34, 36, 39, 40, 42, 44, 52
growth, 51
guardian, 46
guerrilla, 41
guilt, 35

H

hands, 5, 12, 25
harvest, 51
hate, 3
head, 38, 39
health, 13, 18
heart, 37
hemisphere, 36
homes, 50
Honda, 23
hospital, 10
hostility, 46, 53
households, 9, 22
human, 7
human rights, 7
humanity, 32
hybrid, 30

I

identity, 12, 40
ideology, vii, 1, 13, 22, 25, 29, 33, 37, 39, 41, 42, 44, 53
images, 37
implementation, 10, 14
incentive, 50
independence, 6, 7, 12, 30, 39
India, 5, 6, 11, 16, 17, 31, 42, 43, 45, 49
Indian, 10, 17
Indians, 49
indicators, 9
indigenous, 17, 31, 42
indoctrination, 4, 5, 25, 32, 37, 44
industry, 10
inert, 9
infrastructure, 2, 6, 44
inherited, 29

initiation, 20
insecurity, 12
insight, 5, 14
inspiration, 35
Institute of Peace, 47
institutions, 12, 34, 40, 47
integration, 29
intelligence, 14, 16, 17, 20, 36
intensity, 5
interference, 42
international, 14, 27
internationalism, 31
interpretation, 36, 45
intervention, 6, 11
interview, 16, 18
investment, 50
Iran, 53
Islam, 3, 4, 13, 23, 25, 29, 30, 31, 32, 33, 35, 36, 37, 38, 41, 42, 45, 46, 47, 49, 51
Islamic, 2, 3, 4, 8, 9, 20, 22, 25, 29, 30, 31, 32, 33, 35, 36, 37, 38, 39, 40, 41, 42, 43, 45, 50, 51, 52, 53
Islamic movements, 25
Islamism, 4, 30
isolation, 10

J

Jews, 41, 46
jihad, 3, 4, 18, 19, 23, 24, 25, 29, 32, 33, 34, 36, 44, 45, 46, 52, 55
Jihadi, 1, 2, 15, 17, 19, 21, 23, 24, 25, 29, 34, 48
Jirga, 7, 8, 10, 42
journalists, 25
Judiciary, 7
Jun, 39
jurisdiction, 8
justice, 8, 10, 36

K

Kashmir, 17, 25, 34, 53
killing, 36, 50, 52

L

labour, 38
land, 10, 40, 50
language, 48
law, 7, 8, 10, 11, 22, 42
law enforcement, 8
laws, 7, 8, 9
lawyers, 53
lead, 12, 24
leadership, 20, 33, 35, 41, 46, 49
learning, 42, 45
liberal, 13, 42
lifestyle, 41
limitations, 37
linguistic, 11, 12
linkage, 53
links, 34, 52, 55
literacy, 9
literature, 24, 32
livestock, 9
long distance, 1
loyalty, 9

M

magazines, 17
mainstream, 1, 2, 13, 36
mainstream society, 2, 13
maintenance, 10
males, 9
marches, 30
markets, 42
meanings, 37, 48
measures, 7, 26
mechanical, iv
media, 14, 37, 40, 49
membership, 25, 31
memory, 6, 22
men, 3, 15, 16, 19, 37, 38, 43
mentor, 43, 47
metamorphosis, 34
militant, 1, 2, 12, 13, 24, 25, 34, 37, 39, 40, 41, 42, 44
military, 13, 15, 16, 19, 21, 26, 32, 34, 47, 53

millennium, 24, 34
minorities, 36
minority, 42
missions, 20
MMA, 33
modalities, 31
modernization, 13
money, 18, 19, 22, 41, 43, 44, 50, 51
money markets, 42
Mongols, 6
morals, 12
moths, 19
mountains, 18, 19
movement, 4, 11, 15, 19, 20, 22, 23, 30, 32, 34, 36, 43, 44, 45, 46
Mujaheddin, 39
multiculturalism, 46
murder, 53
music, 13, 38
Muslim, 3, 4, 25, 29, 30, 31, 33, 37, 38, 43, 45, 52, 53
Muslim states, 33
Muslims, 30, 33, 38, 39, 42, 45
mutiny, 45

N

nation, 29, 30
national, 5, 51
nationalism, 25, 27, 31
nationality, 33
natural, 41
neglect, 37
network, 23, 26, 34, 39, 43, 45
New World, 3
New York, 12, 15, 16, 43
New York Times, 15, 16
NGO, 40
non-Muslims, 38
norms, 7, 36
nuclear, 2, 55
nucleus, 25, 36, 42

O

obligation, 38

opposition, 9, 34, 45
organization, 3, 14, 21, 23, 25, 26, 30, 32, 50, 52
organizations, 4, 23, 24, 30, 43, 45, 50
orthodox, 45
Osama bin Laden, 22, 40, 43, 52

P

Pakistan, iv, vii, 1, 2, 3, 4, 5, 6, 8, 9, 11, 12, 13, 14, 15, 16, 17, 19, 20, 21, 22, 23, 24, 25, 26, 29, 30, 33, 34, 35, 36, 39, 41, 43, 44, 45, 46, 47, 49, 50, 51, 52, 53, 55
Pakistani, vii, 1, 3, 7, 8, 10, 11, 13, 14, 15, 16, 17, 18, 20, 21, 23, 24, 26, 30, 32, 34, 36, 41, 44, 45, 50, 53
paramilitary, 10, 12, 32
partition, 11, 31
partnerships, 46
Pashtun, 5, 7, 9, 40, 42, 44, 45, 46, 53
Pashtunwali, 9, 47, 50
pastoral, 9
pedagogical, 3
pedigree, 51
perceptions, 3
permeation, 14
Persia, 37
personal, 18, 20, 31, 48
philosophy, 38, 44
physicians, 53
planning, 21, 51
polarized, 37
political, 1, 4, 7, 8, 12, 26, 30, 31, 34, 35, 37, 42, 46, 47, 49, 55
political stability, 1
politics, 5, 22, 30, 31, 33, 35, 42
poor, 9, 47
population, 16, 19, 40, 51
porous, 11
porous borders, 11
portfolios, 52
poverty, 9, 13, 50
poverty line, 50
power, 7, 8, 10, 13, 33, 35, 40, 46, 47, 48, 53
powers, 7, 8
prayer, 33
preference, 48
preparedness, 26
president, 17, 39
President Bush, 20
pressure, 21
production, 51
progressive, 37
property, 7, 24
protected areas, 12
proxy, 6
public, 12, 25, 32, 50
public education, 50
public opinion, 32
public view, 12

R

race, 6, 31, 33
radical, 12, 13, 14, 20, 25, 31, 35, 37, 41, 43
radicalism, 5, 29, 46, 53
radio station, 40
reading, 19
reality, 3, 19, 46, 55
recovery, 33
recruiting, vii, 12
refuge, 18, 52
refugee camps, 45
refugees, 18, 52
regional, 1, 14, 19, 26, 56
regular, 12
regulations, 7, 8
rejection, 31, 37
relationship, 43, 46
relatives, 18, 21
religion, 4, 13, 30, 32, 42, 46
religious, 1, 4, 11, 13, 24, 30, 33, 34, 36, 37, 38, 39, 40, 41, 42, 43, 45, 46, 47, 48, 49, 50, 53, 55
reparation, 37
research, vii, 14, 46
researchers, 14, 35
resentment, 5
resistance, 23, 39
resources, 10, 17, 48
retribution, 20
revolt, 26

rhetoric, 22
right to die, 18
righteousness, 31
rigidity, 38
rural, 4, 50
rural areas, 50
Russia, 3, 22, 26
Russian, 6, 41

S

sacrifice, 24
Salafi religious ideology, 1
sanctions, 10
satellite, 23
Saudi Arabia, 48
scepticism, 21
school, 4, 23, 29, 42, 45, 46, 50
science, 37
scientific, 33
search, 11
secret, 15, 34
Secretary General, 15
secular, 44
security, 3, 20, 48, 56
seeds, 24, 34
segmentation, 31
segregation, 13
separate identities, 23
separation, 42
services, 15, 18, 48
shape, 29
shaping, 3, 22, 29
Sharia, 3, 14, 42, 50
sharing, 10
shelter, 11, 47
Shiite, 41
Shiites, 45
siblings, 50
signs, 14
similarity, 32, 33
small-scale business, 9
smuggling, 9, 10
social, 1, 8, 9, 12, 13, 35, 36, 37, 42
social change, 1, 13, 35
social fabric, 1

social justice, 36
social life, 37, 42
social status, 9
social structure, 35
society, 1, 4, 8, 10, 11, 12, 13, 14, 20, 22, 41, 42, 50, 52
soil, 27
South Asia, 45
sovereignty, 11, 31
spelling, 48
spiritual, 1, 33, 45, 46, 47
sporadic, 14, 18
stability, 1, 27, 36
standards, 13, 31
state control, 51
strain, 44
strains, 39, 42
strategic, 1, 14, 25
strength, 16, 21, 22, 24, 26, 42, 51, 55
stress, 31
strikes, 33
stroke, 35
students, 19, 22, 34, 45, 47, 50, 52
subsidies, 6
subsistence, 9, 47, 50, 51
suicidal, 13
suicide, 2, 12
suicide bombers, 2, 12
summer, 18
Sunni, 25, 42, 45
Sunnis, 40
supply, 16
surgeons, 53
surprise, 15, 51
suspects, 20
symbiont, 43
sympathetic, 17
syntax, 48
systematic, 9
systems, 37, 41, 43

T

tactics, 4
takeover, 46

Taliban, i, iii, iv, vii, 2, 3, 4, 5, 14, 15, 16, 17, 18, 20, 21, 22, 23, 24, 25, 26, 29, 30, 32, 35, 36, 37, 39, 40, 41, 42, 43, 44, 45, 47, 48, 49, 50, 51, 52, 53, 55
tanks, 14
targets, 52
taxes, 10
tea, 23
teaching, 45
teens, 23
temporal, 1
tension, 4, 5, 34
tenure, 47
territorial, 7
territory, 7, 16, 19, 21
terrorism, 1, 3, 13, 29, 37, 51, 52
terrorist, 13, 21, 37
terrorists, 12
threat, 1, 13, 38, 45, 52
threats, 14, 26
time, 2, 3, 8, 14, 15, 17, 19, 26, 32, 34, 37, 43, 44, 49, 51, 52, 53
Timur Lane, 6
tolerance, 1
tradition, 9, 21, 40
training, 15, 23, 25, 32, 34, 43, 47, 48, 53
traits, 37
transition, 12
translation, 32
travel, 37
trend, 14, 36, 37
trial, 10
tribal, vii, 1, 2, 5, 6, 7, 8, 9, 11, 12, 13, 14, 16, 17, 18, 19, 20, 22, 24, 25, 26, 31, 39, 40, 43, 52, 53, 55
tribalism, 4, 42
tribes, 5, 6, 8, 11, 17, 39, 40, 42
trucks, 16
tuition, 51

U

UK, 45, 46
UN, 15
unfolded, 26
United States, 19, 25, 48
unmarried men, 38
urban, 1, 4, 12, 13, 14

V

variance, 10
variation, 4
village, 19, 23, 42
violence, 9, 13
violent, 14
vision, 23
voice, 46

W

war, 2, 16, 22, 23, 36, 42, 44, 50
War on Terror, 55
warfare, 34, 39
warlords, 2, 4, 36, 43, 55
Washington, 18, 19, 56
Washington Post, 18
water, 10
watershed, 42
watersheds, 46
Waziristan, 2, 11, 15, 17, 21, 35, 39, 40, 50
weakness, 35
wealth, 7
weapons, 9, 16, 18
wear, 13
whey, 44
wind, 49
winter, 19
women, 12, 13, 37, 45
wool, 37
workers, 24, 33
wrongdoing, 9

Y

young men, 3, 15